The Lazy Paleo Enthusiast's Cookbook

A Collection of Practical Recipes and Advice on How to Eat Healthy, Tasty Food While Spending as Little Time in the Kitchen as Possible

By
Sean Robertson

Table of Contents

Part 1:
Basic Principles, Assorted Practical Advice, and Other (Hopefully Useful) Ideas

Part 2:
A Selection of Practical Recipes Suitable for Lazy, Hedonistic Cavepersons

Part 1:

Basic Principles, Assorted Practical Advice, and Other (Hopefully Useful) Ideas

An Introduction That You May Actually Get Something Out of Reading

In my opinion, literally the only thing that stops most people from eating healthy food is that cooking fucking sucks and takes too long.

Allow me to explain.

When someone sets out to make themselves healthier (or some related goal like losing weight), they seem to encounter a lot of barriers that make it harder for them to achieve their goal.

Some of these perceived barriers, although popular and often cited by "health experts", are mostly imaginary:

- Healthy food doesn't actually cost that much more than junk food - see for yourself by comparing the cost of dinner at your local McDonald's vs. the cost of ground beef at your local grocery store.
- Eating healthy doesn't require you to eat bland or uninteresting food – if you're into eating paleo, you know that tofu and rice cakes aren't required (or encouraged).

- Unless your idea of healthy eating is raw vegan food, you can eat healthy or semi-healthy at 90% of your local restaurants.
- Eating healthy doesn't require calorie counting, food weighing, measuring macronutrient ratios, etc.

And the list goes on.

Honestly, even the widespread lack of credible health information is not the main cause of America's atrocious health. It *is* ridiculous that government health authorities are telling people to avoid fat, do a bunch of jogging, eat huge amounts of whole grains, and other harmful nonsense. This (well-intentioned) misinformation certainly needs to be dealt with and corrected.

But let's be honest: most Americans aren't fat and sickly because they're eating too many whole grains. They're fat and sickly because they know sugar is bad for them, they know processed food is unhealthy, they know green vegetables are important, and so on ... but they keep eating like shit anyway. If the average American ate the diet they *thought* was healthy, it still wouldn't be a great diet, but at least we'd have a population that ate less sugar, more vegetables, and occasionally moved around a little. Despite being an imperfect solution, even these basic things would go a long way.

So if we all know approximately what food to eat in order to become healthier, why do Americans voluntarily continue their gradual transformation into sick, bloated, cancerous, diabetic manatees?

It's because (as you may recall from the beginning of this introduction) cooking fucking sucks and takes too long.

Or, if you want to put it more precisely and with less vulgarity - the perceived effort-to-reward ratio of cooking is too low.

An example is in order.

Frozen pizza isn't gourmet food by any stretch of the imagination, but the cheese, salt, white flour, and other ingredients that it contains stimulate our brains' pleasure centers surprisingly well, so from the standpoint of our physical and sensory enjoyment of our food, the "reward" value of frozen pizza is fairly high.

Likewise, the process of actually cooking frozen pizza is so easy it could be done by a coma patient, so the amount of required "effort" that frozen pizza requires is low.

This is the effort-to-reward ratio.

There are counter-examples with healthy food. People rarely eat green vegetables, for example, because generally speaking greens taste bland or bitter. A bowl of broccoli has the advantage of being easy to prepare (low effort), but it also tastes mediocre (low reward). And incorporating that broccoli into a tasty Thai stir-fry is delicious (high reward) but also more time-consuming and less convenient (high effort).

Low effort + high reward = food people want to eat.

When someone says (for example) "I don't have time to cook", what they mean is "the perceived effort-to-reward ratio of cooking is too low". Time isn't the real issue – the fact that the average American watches several hours of TV per day (Nielsen data from 2010 puts the average at 34 hours per week), makes it abundantly clear that the necessary time exists. Likewise, cooking a simple meal at home takes 15-20 minutes, which is pretty much the same as the amount of time it takes to drive to a fast food joint. The difference here is that cooking feels like work, while going to get fast food feels like a fun indulgence. The effort is technically the same in both scenarios, but the *perceived* effort is much different.

What this means is that for those of us who are interested in improving our health, one of the highest-yield activities we can engage in is improving the effort-to-reward ratio of our food.

The way we do this is by A) increasing how enjoyable our food is, and B) decreasing the effort required to make that food.

This book is designed to help you do both.

The recipe section, for example, is devoted to recipes that, in my opinion taste awesome (increasing the reward value of our food) and are also very easy to prepare (decreasing effort). Other sections of this book contain little tricks and bits of advice that in various ways make food taste better, last longer, easier to make, less expensive, etc. All of which helps us tip the effort-to-reward ratio more and more in our own favor.

I don't consider anything in this book particularly definitive concerning diet or cooking; it's more of a collection of my own little personal experiments and findings that I think will be helpful to people like me (i.e. people who want to eat food that is healthy and tastes great but don't want to spend a lot of time in the kitchen). Since everyone on the planet has widely different goals, lifestyles, and preferences, I would never suggest that anyone follow the advice in this book verbatim. Instead, I consider this to be more of a "choose-your-own-adventure" type of book, where you try everything that appeals to you and quickly abandon anything that doesn't.

The only reason I feel justified in writing this book in the first place is because I feel like my own research and trial-and-error experiments have ended up putting me in a pretty amazing position. Since going paleo, I'm happy to say that I now have tons of physical energy, I never get sick, and I feel awesome. I get to eat bacon, dark chocolate, steak, blueberries with coconut milk, and other amazing, indulgent food every day – rather than sacrificing hedonism for health (or vice versa), I get to have both. And on top of the fact that everything I eat tastes awesome and makes me feel like a million bucks, I hardly spend any time in the kitchen.

So, even though I'm not a fan of offering advice to strangers, the fact that I've gotten to such a happy place with my diet makes me feel like it would be helpful to throw a few ideas out there for my fellow paleo enthusiasts to experiment with.

You'll notice that I stress this whole "self-experimentation" thing quite a bit throughout the book. Honestly, it's probably going to get to the point where it gets tedious to read. But this is a deliberate choice on my part: personal experimentation is the ultimate test of what works for you and what doesn't.

My intention isn't to tell anyone what to do, but to share some ideas I've found extremely helpful, in the hopes that you'll use them merely as convenient starting points for your own mad-scientist-style experiments in the kitchen.

So, in the spirit of personal experimentation and sharing ideas, let me share with you some of the concepts that I use on a daily basis to make my food healthier, easier, and tastier. I sincerely hope you find these little ideas helpful, and get as much use out of them as I do.

A Few Things You Might Like to Know About Me and Where I'm Coming From With This Whole "Healthy Eating" Thing

To start with, I'll tell you a few things about myself in relation to my views on food and health in general, so that you know where the advice in this book is coming from.

If you don't give a rat's ass about my background, you're welcome to skip this section, but I think it's helpful to know about the personal views and philosophies of anyone who you're considering getting advice from, so I think it would be helpful for you to know a little about my background.

All of the following tidbits don't relate directly to each other, except for the fact that they're all about my background as it relates to food and physical health.

Some are fairly personal (for example, there are two sections below that deal with my feelings on veganism and animal rights issues), and likely to offend some people. So if you're the kind of person who regularly gets offended by reading other people's opinions, you might want to skip this part of the book and move on to the parts where I talk about fun recipes and stuff.

Without further ado...

...

To start with, I'm not dogmatic about paleo advice at all, as you'll see throughout this book. Depending on the situation, I'm comfortable using small amounts of all kinds of foods that would make a paleo Nazi blush, like raw honey, peanut butter, dried fruit, potatoes, tomatoes, dairy, etc.

Everyone has their own hang-ups in the paleo community, so odds are that half of those foods seem fine to you and the other half made you cringe in horror – suffice it to say that when I depart from paleo dogma, I have very strategic reasons for doing so. I ruthlessly self-experiment to determine what impact various foods have on my health and vitality, so I know what works and what doesn't for my personal physiology and lifestyle.

In my view, if I have a little protein powder flavored with sucralose, some mayo, and some commercially-produced sweet potato fries that were fried in vegetable oil, in a given week I'm still way ahead of 99% of the population. So I don't think my diet is going to kill me anytime soon. The fact that I'm healthy, full of energy, and strong as an ox would seem to bear out my hypothesis, but if you want to be really strict about your diet, go ahead.

...

To further alienate any paleo Nazis reading this, I'll also mention that I take a "day off" from eating healthy once per week, in which I basically go out of my way to eat copious amounts of junk food all day long and make an all-around pig of myself.

There actually is a small mount of benefit to this: because of the short, intense spike of sugar and calories, this once-a-week junk food binge actually has some minimal positive effects on leptin levels, sex hormone production, muscle glycogen stores, metabolism, etc. These benefits are small, but the main benefit is psychological – spending one day per week eating filthy, glorious junk food is a lot of fun, and it makes it very easy for me to not eat junk the other six days of the week. It also means when I eat junk food, I really enjoy it and savor it: the fact that I only eat sugar and white bread once per week makes them delicious and kind of "special" and fun, rather than being just ordinary, everyday comfort foods like they are when they're consumed regularly.

These psychological benefits are particularly helpful for people who are dieting for fat loss (which tends to be noticeably more restrictive than regular maintenance-level healthy eating), but everyone who eats healthy can benefit from this kind of periodic hedonistic release.

This once-a-week day off is definitely not ideal from a health standpoint, and there are certainly other ways that things like carb re-feeds and cyclical calorie surpluses can be accomplished that don't involve eating a pile of donuts for breakfast followed by an entire pizza for lunch and a pint of Ben and Jerry's. But personally, I haven't noticed any particular negative effects on my health or energy levels since I first implemented this habit, and more importantly, this weekly junk food binge is super fun and makes me happy. Which is pretty much why we all got into this whole "healthy eating" thing in the first place.

...

At the time of this writing, I'm not particularly hung up on whether the food I eat is organic or not. This isn't because I think organic food is bogus, it's because I genuinely have no idea one way or the other.

I suspect that the organic food movement is a little over-blown, but that at the very least there's a grain of truth to it. Beyond that, I'm not prepared to make a conclusive decision on the issue yet, because I just don't currently have the time to give this topic the amount of research it deserves.

There are people on both sides of the issue who are very sure of their position, cite lots of academic data in favor of their arguments, etc, so I don't want to make any assumptions without careful research. And due to my nature, when I decide that I'm going to research a complex issue like this, I feel the need to really dig in and devote a lot of time to it, which I'm not currently able to do.

A lot of my food ends up being organic or near-organic anyway, since a lot of the food that I like (coconut oil, almond butter) or feel ethically compelled to buy (pasture-raised animal products) is only available at health food stores, co-ops, and other hippy establishments that only sell organic food. So despite the fact that I'm not currently super gung-ho about organic food, I may be accidentally saving my health and the environment anyway.

Also, I don't wear any "organic clothing" or anything like that. I feel great in my non-organic clothes, so I'm not particularly worried about my underpants slowly poisoning me to death.

Regardless of whether the organic food thing turns out to be important or not, I think we can all agree that priority number one is eating healthier *types* of food, not just switching over to the organic version of the same crap we're already eating. Organic cookies aren't as healthy as non-organic spinach, and it's somewhat silly for us to be arguing about this issue while third world countries don't have *any* food (organic or otherwise) and most Americans still haven't figured out how to get by on less than a liter per day of Diet Coke.

If you like organic food, by all means continue to enjoy it. You may be right about how great it is. Just ignore the parts of this book where I talk about buying evil non-organic ingredients, and we'll get along swimmingly.

...

I don't drink filtered water, I drink tap water. Inexplicably, this reckless habit has not caused me to mutate into a tentacled monster.

If you want to filter your water, buy one of those large, inexpensive water-filter jugs for your house. I've used one in the past, and it was both very easy and very inexpensive (replacing the filter costs about $2 per month when you average it out).

If you buy bottled water, you need to stop. Contrary to what the label implies, bottled water comes from the same municipal water supply that your tap water comes from; feel free to read the fine

15

print on the label to verify this. Even if the water comes from someplace like France, it's pretty much just French tap water. Buy a water-filter jug, and spend all the extra money you save on charity donations or an attractive prostitute.

...

For convenience, I do about 70% of my shopping at Whole Foods and the remaining 30% at local co-ops.

For this reason, I'm going to be mentioning ingredients that I buy at Whole Foods several times throughout this book. This is just because that's where I typically find them, not because I care where you buy your groceries.

...

Animal treatment issues are extremely important to me. I'm a actually a former vegan, and the reason why I first became vegan wasn't because I thought it would make me healthier, but because I was (and still am) horrified by the way animals are treated in the factory farm system.

Although I'm no longer vegan or even vegetarian, animal treatment issues are still extremely important to me, and I'm fairly strict about making sure that the animal products that I consume come from animals that have been raised as humanely as possible.

I'm going to briefly be preachy about this; feel free to skip this section if you don't care.

Briefly: it constantly amazes me how often people in the paleo community talk about the benefits of pasture-raised animal products in terms of nutrient content, Omega 3:6 ratios, etc, rather than in terms of preventing animals from spending most of their lives in a pool of their own feces or being castrated without anesthetic. I don't want to spend a lot of time on this point, I just want to point out that as far as I'm concerned, the extra nutrients in the meat are a free bonus, not the most important thing.

I won't bore you with the details of how I arrived at my current set of opinions about what I consider "ethical" when it comes to animal treatment, or what my personal "rules" are concerning the food I eat. My diet definitely isn't perfect, so I don't deserve to say much more on the subject. I'd just like to see the see the topic of ethics brought up more when people discuss their eating habits, regardless of whether or not anyone agrees with me.

...

Related to the above: unlike a lot of ex-herbivores, I actually had a really good experience as a vegan. I was a "raw vegan" (look it up if you don't know what that is), which meant that I didn't suffer from all the problems that normal vegans encounter when they replace the meat in their diet with a bunch of grain, soy, and processed imitation meats.

I won't bore you with details about how I transitioned out of it. I'll just say that even though I think raw foodism (and veganism in general) is misguided, I would highly encourage anyone to try it out for a month just as a light-hearted thought experiment. It will give you a new level of understanding for all the herbivores that you'll meet throughout your life.

…

At the time of this writing, I'm currently eating for fat loss, in order to support certain athletic goals that I have (I'm currently quite lean, but I'm aiming for sub-10% body fat, basically to improve my strength-to-weight ratio).

I bring this up for two reasons:

If you're currently aiming for fat loss (specifically with a low-carbohydrate version of the standard paleo diet), a bunch of the recipes in this book will still work really well for you.

Likewise, if you're an athlete, bodybuilder, or sports devotee, you can rest assured that these recipes have all been field-tested on myself during periods where I've been exercising as much as 9-10 hours per week.

Basically, the vast majority of the recipes in this book should be be usable by anyone, regardless of their current health and fitness goals.

…

And finally, before I stop talking about myself, there's one more topic that deserves some discussion...

How I Feel About Various Paleo-Controversial Foods

If you're getting impatient for some bacon recipes, you can go ahead and skip this section. But if you want to know why I use certain foods in my cooking, read on.

There's typically a fair amount of debate in the paleo community about "gray area" foods - the 20% or so of foods that are not conclusively good for you or bad for you.

Pretty much everyone who's into paleo agrees that foods like grains and sugar are almost always bad, even if you eat a "high-quality" version such as sprouted grains, organic evaporated cane juice, etc.

By the same token, we can all agree that foods like meat, eggs, and green vegetables are almost always categorically great, even if you don't buy the highest-quality version (organic / local / grass-fed / whatever).

However, depending on where you lie on the spectrum of paleo opinions, you may be staunchly for or against foods like potatoes, beans, dairy, tomatoes, peanuts, and so on.

And on top of all this, there are some foods that everyone agrees are okay to eat in certain amounts, but there's disagreement on exactly what amount is recommended / allowable.

This book is not designed to be a discussion of what's healthy. There's already a ton of excellent information out there for you to consult about the effects of various foods and substances on human health. So I'm not going to go all biology-teacher on you.

I also don't think anyone should try and give definitive prescriptive guidelines to strangers. To a large degree, individual eating guidelines can only be determined by taking into account things like individual food sensitivities, allergies, genetic and lifestyle factors, athletics goals, and (most importantly) rigorous personal experimentation.

Basically, whether or not a food can be called "good for you" is sometimes very clear-cut (i.e. refined sugar is bad, leafy green vegetables are good) and sometimes very situation-dependent (i.e. sweet potatoes are great for replenishing muscle glycogen after weight training, but probably not ideal for weight loss).

Related to this, the reason why a lot of people criticize certain foods is because *they* have a sensitivity to those foods, not because *everyone* has a sensitivity to those foods.

For example, most of us (possibly as many as 75%, by some estimates) have trouble digesting dairy to some degree. But it would be pretty self-centered for us to label dairy as "unhealthy" for the other 25% of the world, just because most of us don't tolerate it well.

Plenty of other examples abound. People who don't like fruit very much tend to recommend keeping fruit consumption low, people who don't like beans recommend avoiding beans, etc. This doesn't necessarily mean they're wrong, but it's important to acknowledge our own personal biases when we're evaluating whether a food is objectively healthy or not.

Which is exactly why I'm going to talk about my own personal views on food selection in this section - not for the purpose of telling you what to eat, but so that you know why I've chosen the particular eating habits, recipes, and other approaches that are discussed elsewhere in this book.

I can't stress this point enough: this is not intended to get anyone to eat the way I do. I'm going to criticize a few paleo dogmas I disagree with, but it's up to you to test these assumptions for yourself.

Basically, if I use certain foods that you consider questionable, I want you to know why.

I strongly encourage you to self-experiment and draw your own conclusions (if eating something makes you feel bad, then obviously don't eat it,even if it's "healthy").

But before you self-experiment, I want you to understand a little bit of the theoretical framework that I use when I make decisions about what I put in my mouth. Insert your own inappropriate joke here, you perv.

With that out of the way, my feelings on paleo-controversial foods are as follows:

Fruit

I have heard more than one person in the paleo community refer to fruit as being "bags of sugar and water", or some similar phrasing. To me, this sounds like something that only a person with and eating disorder would say.

Yes, I know that the fructose in fruit is chemically no different from the fructose found in refined sugar and HFCS.

Yes, I know that modern fruit has been genetically bred for artificially high sweetness and sugar content.

And yes, I agree that minimizing sugar (no matter the source) is definitely one of the most important things to do from a health standpoint.

None of these facts mean that we should be worried about eating an apple.

From an observational standpoint, there are healthy, long-lived populations all over the planet that subsist largely on fruit with no apparent ill effects.

From a biochemical standpoint, fruit is nutrient-dense, and very low in sugar compared to almost all modern foods.

It's certainly important to acknowledge that fruit is unnecessary. Although fruit has very good micronutrient content, tastes lovely, and is often a very convenient and helpful food group to include in your diet, the way the mainstream media hypes it up is also overblown. It's silly to treat fruit like candy, but it's equally silly for mainstream health experts to have such an enormous hard-on for the stuff. If you're reading this book, you're probably aware of the fact that the human body's daily requirement for fruit is zero, so I won't belabor the point further.

Fruit is probably not good for fat loss – this may be because of the fructose content, which converts to fat very readily, or because the sweetness creates some palatability and food-reward issues. Regardless of the mechanism, a lot of people report stalled fat loss if they include fruit in their diet, so if you're looking to drop a few pounds, you might want to experiment with cutting it out of your diet. But it's important to recognize that you're only doing this as a fat loss trick, and that it in no way improves your health.

Eat fruit if you like it, and don't eat it if you don't.

Dairy

As mentioned previously, most of us have some degree of digestive issue with dairy, which is exactly why we should all experiment with A) removing dairy completely from our diets for a short period of time, and then B) reintroducing various kinds of dairy to see what agrees with us.

I've never heard of anyone who had an issue with butter, probably because it's mostly fat. I've also noticed that I can eat small amounts of Greek yogurt with no trouble, possibly because of the fermentation. So butter is probably fine to leave in your diet, and other forms of dairy can be included on a case by case basis.

I've also heard some personal accounts of people who stopped eating grain, fixed their gut bacteria, etc, and were able to tolerate dairy just fine after that. These examples highlight the importance of personal experimentation.

Personally I keep dairy to a minimum, other than a little bit of Greek yogurt and occasionally small amounts of mayo used in certain recipes. A lot of very viable dairy substitutes exist out there, so it's easy to avoid if you have a lot of trouble with it, as long as you stay away from the soy milk.

Honey

From what I understand, honey (even the raw, unprocessed kind) is pretty much pure sugar, so I keep it to a minimum. But I'm not afraid of having a few grams of sugar in my diet, so when I do consume something sweetened, I use raw honey, It actually does contain some nutrient content, and is almost completely unprocessed, which can't be said for any other sweetener I'm aware of.

It's true that honey isn't healthy just because it's "natural", but it's also true that small amounts of sugar are going to "ruin your insulin resistance" or whatever. So I'm not afraid of a little honey, even though I rarely hear about anyone in the paleo community using it.

Artificial Sweeteners

I treat fake sugar pretty much like real sugar. I strongly curtail my use of it, but I don't freak out about using it occasionally.

Artificial sweetener is definitely, 100% not a healthy substance – the reason why it goes in the gray zone is not because it's sometimes healthy, but because it can often be useful in small amounts as a strategically useful replacement for refined sugar (such as for people doing the low-carb thing for fat loss).

Since I hate the way most artificial sweetener tastes, I rarely use it, but a few times per week I may use it in certain contexts.   Currently, on workout days I like to mix a little chocolate protein powder (which contains sucralose) with some unflavored Greek yogurt, just as a tasty little dish that adds some protein to my diet and won't negatively affect my fat loss too much.

The reason I bring this up is to point out that in actual practice, there's a big difference between adding a little protein powder to some healthy, full-fat, probiotic-rich Greek yogurt, as opposed to knocking back a Diet Coke.   Context is always important, even with something that is clearly unhealthy when viewed in isolation, like artificial sweetener.

Beans

I avoid them personally, but I don't think it's a big deal for people to eat them.   From what I understand, the antinutrient content in beans and legumes is definitely non-optimal, but it can also be significantly reduced by soaking (which happens automatically with canned beans).

I pretty much never eat them, because A) the antinutrient content is potentially troubling, B) their micronutrient content doesn't particularly impress me compared to other foods, and C) I don't find them especially tasty or convenient.

So I currently have no particular problem with beans, but consider them a marginal food that's not worth including in my diet.

Peanuts

I haven't done much experimenting with peanuts, but currently I almost never consume them. They apparently have a moderate amount of antinutrients, and are clearly inferior to other nuts in terms of their micronutrient profile. Since almonds (including things like almond butter) can be used for almost everything that peanuts can be used for, I just eat almond products, because I find them equally convenient and they're almost definitely healthier.

If you're a total whore for peanut butter, try alternating it every other week with almond butter and see what happens.

Nuts in general

I try to keep nuts fairly minimal in my diet, but recognize their usefulness.

On the plus side, they frequently have a nice micronutrient profile, not to mention their portability, long shelf life, etc. Unfortunately, the protein in nuts isn't as biologically useful to our bodies as animal protein, and the Omega 6 content is potentially problematic. So there are arguments both for and against nuts as a "health food". Just to be on the safe side, I keep my nut consumption fairly low and just treat them like a semi-healthy convenience.

I also make sure to buy roasted nuts, rather than raw ones. From what I understand, roasting and soaking are useful processes for deactivating the enzyme inhibitors found in most nuts, so if I can find a roasted version of a particular kind of nut, I favor that over the raw version.

I've tried soaking raw nuts, but in my experience it gives them a weird texture that I don't like, so roasting it is.

I'm also fairly careful to check the label on the nuts that I buy; salted nuts are easy to spot, but a lot of stores sell nuts roasted in hydrogenated vegetable oils, so it's something worth watching out for.

Potatoes

I pretty much never eat potatoes, but I also consider them wrongfully-maligned in the paleo community.

A lot of people put forward the idea that sweet potatoes are better than the common white potatoes, but I haven't seen much practical evidence to back that up. Both are starchy tubers with comparable macronutrient ratios, and both offer comparable amounts of various micronutrients (i.e. the micronutrient composition is different between potatoes, but all varieties conatain useful nutrients).

The only difference between the various potato species, as far as I've been able to determine, is that white potatoes contain glycoalkaloids, which are unhealthy in large amounts. Since most of us don't eat large amounts of potatoes, and since potatoes only contain small amounts of these compounds, *and* since they can be reduced even further by cooking (which everyone does with potatoes anyway) and removing the skin (where most of the glycoalkaloids are apparently concentrated), I don't think this is going to be much of a problem for most of us.

Some people report various levels of intolerance to eating potatoes, which is likely due to a sensitivity to these glycoalkaloids. People with this problem often don't have the same issue with sweet potatoes or yams, so if you're one of these people, you may want to experiment with white potatoes vs. other potatoes to see if you notice any difference.

Some people may also be carbohydrate-sensitive, and should be keeping carbohydrate-rich foods (like tubers and fruit) to a minimum.

Potatoes in general are probably not ideal for weight loss, due to the fact that the starch breaks down into glucose during digestion. But for certain purposes, like replenishing muscle glycogen after weight training, starchy tubers are great. I've also heard that they're helpful for long distance runners and other types of endurance-based athletic pursuits.

The reason why I personally never eat potatoes is because these days I rarely eat any type of starchy tuber (due to the previously-mentioned fat loss experiment that I'm doing). On the rare occasions when I do, it's usually sweet potato fries, just because I love the way they taste.

30

In the future I'll probably do a little more careful side-by-side testing to see if one type of starchy tuber makes me feel better than other types, but for now I suspect that the majority of people (barring any unusual circumstances) can lighten up and enjoy a nice baked potato now and then without ending up homeless on the street giving blowjobs for crack.

Carbohydrates in General

People who are into "low-carb" eating are kind of weird in some ways.

First they argue that a calorie is not just a calorie, and that the source of a person's calories matters much more than just the total number of calories they're eating.

Then they turn around and treat all carbohydrates as if they're the same, and insist that everyone should stay under x number of carbs per day or doom themselves to a life of obesity and heart attacks.

I'm sure that if you asked these people directly, they would admit that an apple is different from a Snickers bar, but a lot of the people who advocate low-carb dieting don't seem to pay much attention to this distinction.

This silliness has a tendency to damage the credibility of an otherwise good idea. Cat this point, carbohydrate restriction has a pretty good track record of helping with weight loss. So regardless of whether researchers think that this is a result of decreased insulin, spontaneous calorie reduction, manipulation of food-reward theory, or whatever, the basic idea seems pretty useful at this point.

That being said, if someone goes low-carb by eating a bunch of processed meat, artificial sweeteners, and crappy cheese made with hydrogenated vegetable oil, they're going to have health problems, and probably screw up their weight loss to boot.

This is especially true if someone gets so focused on using their overall grams-of-carbs-per-day as a metric of health that they forget to eat enough green vegetables, and end up giving themselves a micronutrient deficiency.

Most people who are into paleo probably have enough sense to avoid this problem, but it's worth keeping in mind if you ever find yourself becoming too focused on paper-statistics like how many grams of carbohydrate are in your diet.

With those caveats in mind, I think carbohydrate restriction can potentially be a great tool for weight loss, as long as it's not the only tool you're using. A healthy diet is probably going to end up being fairly moderate in carbohydrates anyway, but for practical reasons (like athletics, weight loss, etc.), carbs can definitely be adjusted up and down with few ill effects either way.

Raw dairy

For most of us, I doubt that raw vs. traditional dairy is as important to our health as dairy vs. no-dairy (based on our personal genetic ability to digest lactose).

There seems to be some indication that raw dairy tends to be superior to pasteurized dairy, so if it's convenient and you want to try it, give it a whirl.

Whenever I use some cheese in a recipe, I pick up a block of raw cheddar from the dairy case at Whole Foods, and it seems to agree with me just fine.

Salt

I don't do well with salt, so I tend to avoid it, along with most foods that contain any noticeable amount of it (with the exception of bacon, which is hard to say no to).

From what I understand, the mainstream tendency to demonize salt for supposedly causing heart attacks has been overblown - the fact that salt is an ingredient in lots of unhealthy foods can create a false correlation between salt and bad health, depending on which observational study you look at.

I've also heard that different people have different tolerance levels for salt, but I haven't researched it much, since I'm a grossly selfish creature who only cares about himself, and I already know how I respond to it.

I've noticed that anything more than a very minimal amount of salt tends to make me tired, and I've heard the same from pretty much everyone who's written on the subject. So I would be pretty confident in recommending that the average person cut down on their salt intake. But if you're a big salt fan, experiment for yourself and see what happens.

Cured Meats

This is partially related to the salt issue, since most cured meat seems to be salted in some capacity (even if it's with "nitrates" rather than ordinary table salt).

I've noticed that eating cured meats in anything more than small quantities tends to make me tired (just like salted foods in general).

I've noticed this particularly with ground meats like salami and pepperoni, even when I get them at hippy-dippy health food stores that have supposedly removed all the unhealthy additives.

I've rarely heard about anyone who does just as well eating cured meats as when they eat regular meats. So personally, I minimize these meats as much as possible, but allow myself liberal amounts of bacon for fun.

Fat

The paleo community seems to be primarily pro-fat (as long as it's not hydrogenated vegetable oil), but a surprising number of paleo people seem to be wary of fat consumption, so it's worth addressing the issue.

I won't go into the various theoretical physiological reasons I've come across that make a strong case for a high-fat diet. I'll just mention that I've personally experimented with various levels of fat consumption (low, moderate, and high), and haven't seen any noticeable improvements from moderating my fat intake.

Currently I eat lots of fat and I feel great, so that's what I'm sticking with.

...

As a final word, if you're on the fence about any of the above foods, keep in mind that you don't need any of them in order to be healthy. The dietary requirement for every single food in this section is literally zero, so the above guidelines aren't really about what's necessary, they're about what's helpful, convenient, or conducive to other types of goals outside the realm of physical health.

So if you feel suspicious of any of the above foods, you can easily omit them from your diet and go on to live a long happy life full of green vegetables and grass-fed beef, without so much as a single orange wedge or potato skin in sight.

...

So now that we've gotten the necessary background information out of the way, let's get down to the nitty-gritty stuff that will keep your lazy ass out of the kitchen.

A Few Basic Principles

There are a lot of little tricks and ideas that I use in order to achieve maximum laziness in food preparation with minimal sacrifice of nutritional value and food enjoyment. In this his section, I'll be discussing some of the most basic principles that I use all the time.

These principles all work together nicely, but they can each be used separately as well, so if one of the ideas in this section doesn't fit your personal preferences, chances are that it can be modified, or ignored entirely.

There are only a few fundamental things that I'll be covering in this section, because they apply to almost all of the cooking and food preparation that I do. More specific, situational tricks are discussed elsewhere in the book.

Let's jump right in, shall we?

Batching

The concept of "batching" is probably the main concept that I base my cooking around. Most of us, back when we were kids, were exposed to a version of this idea by our moms.

My mom, for example, would often take an afternoon and make a week's-worth of dinners all at once. She would parcel them out into little individual meal-sized containers, and then load them into the freezer to be de-thawed as necessary throughout the week. This, in a nutshell, is the principle of batching. Although there are better ways of doing it in my opinion, the idea is that you only do one day of cooking, and then (depending on how you're doing it) you've got anywhere from a few days to a month of pre-cooked food ready to go whenever you want it.

The downside of the approach described above (namely, freezing meals in advance) is that the food often tastes mediocre from being frozen and then de-thawed. This disadvantage, I think, is what prevents most of us from batching our food, because we don't want to constantly be eating leftovers.

So in spite of my aversion to leftovers, I decided to experiment with the concept of batching in an effort to get rid of the unpleasantness of eating crappy de-frosted food every day, while still maintaining the convenience of pre-prepared food.

And the benefits of pre-preparing food are actually pretty substantial in terms of how much time it can save you. Batching, in the broader, non-culinary sense of the term, is actually a widely-applicable productivity technique that can be used for all kinds of different tasks. It involves taking a tedious activity that you have to do on a regular basis, and rather than doing it all the time, you pick one block of time to do a large amount of this tedious work at once. This allows you to be very efficient at the task, because rather than constantly starting and stopping, you allow yourself to get into a groove - you get a bunch of work done in a single session, and then don't have to do that work again for a long time. It's a concept that a lot of businesspeople have applied to tasks like checking email, making sales calls, etc.

Applied to food preparation, batching allows us to go from spending (for example) one hour per day preparing our meals, to spending a single block of 3 hours, once per week, preparing the entire week's-worth of food in advance. Not only is it much more convenient to squeeze all of our weekly cooking into a single day like this, it also cuts down on the *total* amount of cooking time. In the above example, our total weekly cooking time goes from 7 hours (1 hour per day x 7 days) to 3 hours (3 hours per day x 1 day) to prepare exactly the same amount of food.

The above example is a little simplistic – for example, you'll still have to spend at least a few minutes per day heating up the food you've pre-made and stored. You also may not want to make a week's-worth of meals in advance (because you don't want certain foods sitting in your fridge for a week), and so on. The point of the example is to illustrate a principle: if you can concentrate your efforts, you can produce more results in less time.

Batching also provides a happy medium between the two extremes of modern eating. On the one hand, you have convenient junk food, and on the other hand, you have healthy but very time-consuming home-cooked food. Both approaches require tradeoffs (junk food is convenient but unhealthy, and vice versa for home-cooked food)

Batching, when done properly (and there are definitely ways to screw it up, in my opinion) allows you to get all the health benefits of made-from-scratch food, as well as most of the culinary/flavor benefits, while only spending a total of 2-3 hours per week in the kitchen. It's a very powerful compromise.

There are, however, some potential pitfalls and caveats to deal with in order to achieve these benefits. They are as follows:

Food and Recipe Selection - Some foods keep better than others, and some foods keep just fine but taste crappy when they're re-heated.

Selecting the right foods and recipes (or modifying existing recipes using more storage-friendly ingredients), is critical for making sure your food survives it's first night in the fridge.

Timing - Store a dish overnight and it usually tastes fine the next day. Leave it in the fridge for a week and it will probably taste like crap.

With every food, the cut off date for spoilage is going to vary (in some cases drastically), so we need to find the sweet spot between how much food we can prepare in advance vs. how quickly it will start to taste bad.

Storage Method - The technology that we use to store our food obviously affects how it's preserved. Most of this is common sense, but there are a few other factors to consider (freezing vs. refrigerating, separating ingredients, etc.)

I've come up with some personal guidelines that I use to get around these problems:

Food and Recipe Selection

This is the primary area I focus on when it comes to batching my food. If we limit most of our food to certain types of recipes that keep really well, than the rest falls into place.

As an easy starting point, all of the recipes listed in the recipe section of this book were explicitly chosen with batching in mind, so you can start there if you want to begin batching your food. Immediately without having to experiment with your own recipes.

That being said, if you end up liking this batching concept, you'll probably want to experiment with other recipes to see if they're batchable as well, so I'll point out some factors that I've noticed will make a dish particularly storage-friendly.

This isn't an exact science: the simplest and most direct way for determining which recipes work best for batching is just by making a recipe, throwing it in the fridge, and seeing how it holds up over a few days. But in my own experience, I've found that there are a few criteria that seem pretty universal when it comes to evaluating recipes for batchability:

- I've noticed that "mixed" recipes seem to keep very well. The type of recipe I'm referring to here is a dish that just consists of a bunch of ingredients that have all been ground/chopped/diced/pureed/whatever, and then mixed together. Examples from

41

the recipe section of this book include the Paleo Mashed Potatoes, Hamburger Salad, and Bacon Brussels Sprout Slaw. If you look at these recipes, you'll notice that they're basically just a big mix of ingredients in a bowl. I don't know exactly why this type of recipe tends to keep so well, but for some reason most recipes that fit this profile seem to survive well in the fridge.

- Uniform texture also seems to be a good thing. Normally, it's nice from a culinary standpoint for a dish to have a lot of different textures, but I've found that for storage purposes, it's usually best to keep texture relatively simple. For example, if you're eating a salad dish that includes avocado, lettuce, and chicken breast, over time the avocado will get mushy, the lettuce will wilt, and the chicken breast will dry out, and what started as a delightful little medley of texture turns into a squishy, chewy mess. A little texture is fine, but as a rule of thumb, if there's a big range of different textures in the dish, each ingredient will age at a different rate, and the nice textural balance that you started with will be off after a day or two.

- Salads don't work that well, because leafy greens tend to wilt as a result of the moisture found in other ingredients (like meat).

- Dishes that contain a more complex mixture of flavors tend to work well. If the tastiness of the dish hinges on just one flavor, it's all-or-nothing, and if that flavors is off, the flavor of the entire dish is off. But if the dish contains multiple flavors, it doesn't matter if one of those flavors starts to taste a little stale, because the other flavors will kind of "cover" for it.

– Liquid ingredients: the less liquid-y a recipe is, the better it tends to keep. Dishes with lots of liquid content tend to get mushy and spoil more quickly due to the moisture content.

– An exception to the above rule: certain liquid fats can help prolong a dish's life in the fridge. Coconut oil and rendered bacon fat, for example, have very long shelf-lives, so when a dish is coated in these oils, they actually seem to lend some of their long life to the dish and help preserve it.

– Most fruit spoils pretty quickly. Dishes that use dried fruit obviously work fine, but regular fruit turns squishy and unpleasant at the drop of a hat.

Timing

This is a simple one: I've found that about 4 days is pretty much the ideal sweet spot for planning how much food to prepare in advance. For most recipes, if you let the food sit longer than this, it won't necessarily go bad, but it will dry out, toughen up, taste worse, etc. And if you only prepare 2-3 days worth of food in advance, it kind of cuts down on the convenience of batching.

You can go longer if you want; a lot of foods won't actually spoil for a week or so, they'll just start to taste bad. For example, I used to batch my food in six-day increments, because I'm on a six-days-on/one-day-off eating cycle (I eat very healthy six days per week, and use the seventh day as a cheat day). Preparing six days of food at once worked okay, and I never got food poisoning or anything like that, but by the fifth day, the food usually starts to taste old (at least with the recipes I eat most often).

Although a 4-day cycle of cooking obviously doesn't fit neatly into a 7-day week (thanks for nothing, Old Testament), personally I've found it fairly easy to adapt, and it allows for the best balance of convenience and food freshness/tastiness in my experience.

Storage Method

There are a few different ways that you can go with storage methods, so I'll discuss the various factors individually:

- To start with, a commonsense but often-overlooked point: make sure you're using air-tight containers. I prefer using hard plastic containers for this reason – plastic bags tend to develop tiny tears that let air in, and the zippers that hold these bags closed seem to "unlatch" fairly easily. Hard plastic containers also protect your food from getting squished when you put other stuff on top of it.

- When it comes to freezing vs. refrigerating, I find that refrigeration works best for actual dishes. Freezing is great for individual ingredients (which I'll discuss in a moment), but if you'd like to prepare a recipe in advance and then store it, I've found that freezing has a tendency to mess up the food pretty quickly. It will last forever, but since the freezing process physically alters the food (it's frozen solid, after all), it will have a different taste and texture when you thaw it out. Refrigeration isn't perfect, but I've found that it's a little gentler on most recipes that I make.

- When storing a dish that contains sauce (or other liquid ingredients like olive oil, mayo, etc.), it's usually best to store the liquid separately. If you include the liquid from the start and then store the dish in this state, the liquid usually makes the dish soggy and causes it to spoil faster. So separate storage is highly advisable. As mentioned previously, pure fats that don't spoil (like coconut oil, rendered animal fat, etc.) are an exception to this rule, and actually may help extend a dish's shelf life.

- For similar reasons, if you're making a dish that involves leafy greens (like salad), it's better to keep the greens separate during storage, because the moisture from the rest of the ingredients will cause the greens to wilt. Also, if you don't have one already, I highly recommend getting one of those "salad spinner" things for drying off your leafy greens after you wash them – using this appliance gets the leaves way more dry, so they'll last an extra few days before starting to decompose.

...

The above tricks for recipe selection, timing, and storage method, when used together or even individually, will remove the vast majority of problems normally associated with batch-preparing food in advance.

However, no matter how good of a job you do with the batching process, with most recipes you're going to lose a little bit of the flavor (as well as other factors like texture) that you get from fresh-cooked food. You're also going to lose a little bit of the convenience of eating food from a package – it's hard to cut down your prep time to the point where it rivals frozen pizza or candy bars.

But the way I view it, depending on what kinds of strategies you decide to employ, you're going to end up sacrificing 10-20% of the taste of fresh-cooked food, and 10-20% of the convenience of processed food, but you'll be eating the healthiest food possible while simultaneously saving yourself 5-10 hours of food prep time per week. Well worth it, in my distinctly not-humble opinion.

Full-batching vs. Partial-batching

As a last point to wrap up our discussion of this whole batching concept, I'd like to mention the dynamic of full-batching vs. partial-batching.

Full-batching involves making a complete recipe and storing it, so that it can be taken directly out of storage and eaten without additional preparation (other than maybe heating it up in the microwave, pouring on a little sauce, etc).

Partial-batching involves getting a recipe started (preparing all the separate ingredients, marinading meat, or whatever), and then storing it in it's half-finished state, but not actually finishing the dish until just before you're ready to eat. An example of this would be to marinade a week's-worth of meat in advance, but only cook one piece of meat at a time, just before you eat it.

This is a compromise between the convenience of full-batching and the tastiness of cooking from scratch – you save time by preparing all of the ingredients in advance, and then just spend a few minutes before each meal actually cooking the dish or assembling the ingredients. This takes an extra few minutes, but makes the dish taste like it was fresh-cooked.

I've found that meat-based recipes in particular tend to benefit from partial-batching – storing meat in the fridge for more than a day or two usually dries it out and toughens it up. Plant-based recipes seem to have a little more leeway with storage, but when I eat recipes that are mostly meat (like marinaded chicken breasts), these days I usually prefer to partial-batch them.

For people who feel particularly strapped for time, partial-batching may not appeal, but if you think you may have an extra 10 minutes a day to make your food taste better, it's worth considering as an option.

Frozen Ingredients

Frozen foods are massively convenient, but unfortunately most actual dishes (i.e. anything involving more than one ingredient) rarely hold up well in the freezing process. My solution to this: just freeze the individual ingredients until you're ready to use them.

Freezing a dish after it's cooked is what causes the dish to lose it's flavor and texture. But if the ingredients of the dish are all frozen until you're ready to use them, and *then* cooked, it rarely affects the way the final dish turns out.

Freezing ingredients is useful in two ways.

First, it can potentially cut down on the number of trips you have to make to the grocery store in a given month – if you're hardcore about freezing stuff and have a dedicated freezer, you could potentially have a few months'-worth of meat, vegetables, fruit, and other stuff stockpiled in your freezer.

Second, a lot of simple recipes and side dishes can be made on the spot using frozen ingredients. For example, throwing some frozen berries in a blender with some coconut milk makes a nice smoothie, and throwing a bowl of frozen veggies in the microwave makes a nice bowl of veggies.

I'm particularly keen on frozen produce – it's one of those rare food items that is both extremely convenient and fairly inexpensive, while simultaneously being as good or better than the more expensive alternative (fresh produce) in terms of nutrient quality, and even occasionally taste.

Most people who write about health are constantly going on about how important it is to eat "fresh" fruits and vegetables. But fortunately for us, this isn't the case (or, at least, is a massively simplistic statement).

In pretty much all grocery stores, the "fresh" produce actually contains slightly fewer nutrients than the frozen produce. This is due to the fact that frozen fruits and vegetables are flash-frozen immediately after they're harvested, while regular produce can take as much as two weeks to get shipped to the store, and during this time, it's losing nutrients from exposure to light, air, etc. Also, due to the duration of this shipping period, regular produce has to be picked before it's ripe (so that it can ripen during the journey), whereas frozen produce is picked at peak ripeness and flash-frozen in this state. Altogether, this means that frozen fruits and vegetables are pretty much as healthy, if not more so, than the un-frozen stuff.

Note that this doesn't apply to canned produce, which apparently loses a significant amount of its nutrients during the preservation process. And if you're one of those people who buys your produce at farmers' markets (where the farmer just picked it yesterday), then obviously that really is super-fresh, and probably the healthiest option overall (at least by a small margin).

Not only is frozen produce as good as regular produce from the standpoint of nutrition, but as an added bonus, frozen fruits and vegetables can be stored in your freezer for approximately a billion years.

And they're often cheaper to boot. I've particularly found this to be true with berries – maybe it has something to do with their comparative fragility and short shelf life, but for whatever reason, I've found that frozen berries are noticeably less expensive per pound compared to fresh berries.

Personally, I have a stash of frozen broccoli (to be used in recipes or as a side dish) and various frozen berries (to be used in smoothies) in my freezer at all times.

There are certain situations where freshness matters. Frozen spinach, for example, is nowhere near as good as fresh spinach for things like salads, due to the drastic difference in texture between the two. But if you're just going to cook it or throw it in a smoothie, the texture difference will be unnoticeable.

For fruit, fresh fruit is also going to taste way better than frozen fruit if you're eating it on its own (or making some fancy chocolate-covered strawberries or something), because the texture matters a lot in these situations. But again, if you're just throwing it in a blender to make a smoothie, the texture of the fruit ceases to matter, and the frozen stuff will do just as well.

There are other types of frozen foods that can be convenient and fairly healthy (I eat frozen sweet potato fries all the time), so feel free to investigate other options as well.

The moral of the story – frozen foods rock, use them as often as possible.

Foods That Never Expire

The final type of food that needs to be a part of any lazy caveperson's diet is food that never expires.

Yes these foods exist, and they aren't Twinkies. Common paleo examples include almonds, coconut oil, and honey, among others.

In realistic terms, most of these foods will technically go bad if left out long enough, but most of us aren't going to leave a bag of almonds sitting around for a year without touching them, so for practical purposes we can treat them like they have no expiration date.

Examples of foods with very long shelf lives include nuts, seeds, rendered animal fat, various oils (coconut oil, olive oil, etc.), ghee, honey, and dried fruit. Most of these foods fall more in the category of "ingredients", rather than being foods in and of themselves, but they can be combined fairly easily into tasty recipes (for example, see the Fat Mixture and Trail Mix recipes in the recipe section).

These foods also tend to be fairly inexpensive on a per-calorie basis, simply because most of them are very calorie-dense. For example, one cup of almonds contains somewhere around 800 calories, and coconut oil has around 120 calories per tablespoon. Because a lot of these foods are fat-based, they're also very satiating, so you get a lot of bang for your buck.

Obviously not all long-shelf-life foods have these benefits (dried fruit, for example, is neither cheap nor satiating), but the majority of these foods are great for cost-effectiveness as well as long shelf life.

As a nice final bonus, since these foods don't require refrigeration, they tend to be great for travel.

Canned foods deserve an honorable mention in this category as well. Most canned food isn't particularly paleo, butc certain foods (like canned coconut milk or pumpkin puree) are perfectly paleo-compliant and will last until doomsday.

Also worth pointing out: some of the foods on the above list are not ideal from a health standpoint. Nuts tend to be high in omega 6 fatty acids, honey and dried fruit have higher sugar content than we'd prefer, etc. So these foods shouldn't make up the bulk of your diet.

However, because of their massive convenience benefits and their relative healthiness, I've found that making these foods a fairly large *supplementary* part of my diet has been extremely helpful.

...

Just like other aspects of your diet, your level of compliance with these concepts will depend on your tastes, schedule, and lifestyle.

For example, if you're super busy (or super lazy, I suppose), you could certainly figure out a way to batch an entire week's-worth of food at one time, and just bite the bullet and deal with the fact that your food will taste a little old by the sixth or seventh day. And if you're like me, and feel that you have the time and inclination to cook slightly more often, you can do a 4 day cooking cycle, and reap the corresponding benefits of having your food taste a little less stale.

Likewise, I don't currently own a big freezer with a bunch of produce and half a dead cow inside; I still have to go to the grocery store once a week, and I'm comfortable making that sacrifice. But for certain people, having a humongous freezer full of food will be right up their alley.

Experimentation with different foods, recipes, cooking schedules, and storage methods is the only way to determine what will work best for your individual situation, so give some of these ideas a try and see how you like them.

A Note on Appliances

There are probably going to be two main demographics for readers of this book:

1) Knowledgeable cooks who are already fairly experienced in the kitchen, and who just picked this book up for ideas on simplifying their food preparation for times when they're busy, tired, in a hurry, etc.
2) People who are not particularly experienced with cooking, who are put off by complicated recipes, and who quite possibly bought this book specifically because it had the word "lazy" in the title.

This section is probably more for the latter demographic than the former, since most people who are into cooking will probably already have a kitchen full of appliances. Although more experienced foodies may like to read about my experiments with various specialty appliances, and possibly my thoughts on purchasing guidelines, this section will probably be most helpful for people who are just starting out.

Don't feel bad if you fall in this category –
when I started getting interested in healthy eating
(and thus, preparing my own food), the fanciest
appliance I owned was a spork.

The Only Two Appliances I Recommend You Get

When it comes to appliances, there are a
bunch that will waste your time and money, and
two that will make your life drastically easier. The
first, which you probably already own, is a blender,
and the second, which I *hope* you already own, is a
food processor.

I obviously won't spend any time explaining
blenders, since presumably you're over the age of
five and know what they do. If you're like me when
I was in college, and don't even own a freaking
blender, go spend twenty bucks on a cheap one so
that you can start enjoying the benefits of green
smoothies, whole-food protein shakes, non-dairy
mayo, etc.

I also recommend, if you're as cooking-
challenged as I was, that you get a food processor.
These things are massively helpful and very
inexpensive (I think mine cost about $40).

When you're making a week's worth of food
at once, if you don't have a food processor, you may
have to spend 20 minutes chopping, slicing, and
grinding various ingredients if you're doing it by
hand, versus about 2 minutes if you have a food
processor.

It's also great for rapidly mixing recipes that
end up semi-solid (like guacamole, for example), as

opposed to the mostly-liquid concoctions you're limited to with blenders.

Besides the convenience aspect, there are certain things (such as grinding nuts into powder) that you simply can't do by hand, and a food processor can do a lot of these tasks for you.

Both blenders and food processors are extremely versatile and very inexpensive. They're pretty much the only appliances I use in my cooking, and I rarely run into a recipe that requires anything more elaborate or specialized.

Appliances I Tried and Didn't Like

The reason I recommend only the above two appliances isn't because I'm too lazy to use anything else – it's because I've tried a fair amount of kitchen-related junk to see if it would reduce the amount of time I had to spend in the kitchen, and found most of it to be unnecessary.

In order to save you time experimenting (not to mention saving you money buying appliances you don't need), here's a short list of the appliances I tried and didn't like:

Spiral Slicer - This gadget has a few different names, but it's basically a doodad that you feed long thin vegetables into (like cucumbers, zucchini, etc.) and it will spin the vegetable around and slice it up into one long, continuous, spiral-shaped ribbon (look it up if it sounds confusing).

One big use for these things is that with the right attachment, you can take a zucchini and grate/slice it into long, thin strands that resemble pasta noodles. This zucchini pasta is used as a replacement for regular pasta for those of us who are avoiding grain (zucchini is used because A) it fits into the spiral slicer and B) it's fairly bland tasting, just like pasta noodles, which makes it a good base for the pasta sauce).

I was really enthusiastic about this when I first heard about it, because at the time, I was recently converted into raw foodism, and I still missed pasta a lot. It ended up being fairly disappointing, unfortunately.

First, there was a slight vegetable-y taste to the zucchini pasta, which didn't mimic the taste of real pasta as closely as I would have hoped.

More importantly, the texture was all wrong – the zucchini had a certain vegetable-like crispness to it that pasta noodles don't have.

To top things off, zucchini tends to get mushy pretty quickly when stored in the fridge, so it wasn't very good from a convenience/storage standpoint either.

The other uses for the spiral slicer are all basically for fun – if you like salad and want to add some interesting texture to it, you can slice some cucumber/daikon/whatever into little spirals, which I guess is kind of fun and makes the salad's texture more interesting. Personally I'm not a salad guy, so this didn't appeal to me, but if you're into salad or think you might like the taste of zucchini pasta, this might be worth checking out. Personally, I ditched mine and haven't ever missed it.

Dehydrator – another thing I checked out during my raw food period. As a paleo fan, you're probably aware of the fact that dehydrators are used to make dried fruit, beef jerky, etc. They can also be used to make interesting little foods like "fruit leather" and pemmican.

The whole concept sounds pretty cool at first, because (unless you're buying very common foods like raisins) dried fruit can be expensive; last time I checked, dried blueberries and mangoes cost more per pound than black-market human organs. And jerky is notoriously expensive as well.

So not only can a dehydrator hypothetically save you money by allowing you to cut out the middleman and make this stuff yourself, but it also allows you to leave out all the extra crap that manufacturers add (added sweeteners in the case of dried fruit, chemical preservatives in jerky, and so on).

The only downside is that it's a pain in the ass.

Although people on the internet who dehydrate their own food like to talk about how easy it is, personally I didn't find it convenient at all. In order to make dehydrated food, you have to slice up the fruit/meat/whatever you want to dehydrate, season it, and let it dehydrate for 1-2 days.

Depending on your personal tolerances and the amount of pre-existing background noise in the place where you live, the constant hum of the dehydrator running may be annoying.

I also found that you can't just let food dehydrate for a certain number of hours and count on it being done – frequently, I went to check on the food I was dehydrating and found that it wasn't ready yet, so I would have to come back on an hourly basis to keep tabs on it.

Between these various factors, I personally found that it was more convenient, more time-efficient, and less frustrating to pay an extra few bucks for the convenience of buying dehydrated food directly from stores.

Part of the problem could have just been that I bought a fairly inexpensive dehydrator. I'm sure that getting an industrial-strength model allows drying to happen faster, and the larger compartment lets you dehydrate larger batches of food, so maybe the process becomes worth it if you buy a nice one.

I also have no idea whether this home-drying process is efficient from an environmental standpoint. Personally, I always felt kind of guilty letting my dehydrator run overnight just to make the equivalent of a single bowl of food.

After extensive experimentation, I realized that I don't have any particular need for dried food. Dried fruit in particular is tasty but kind of sugary and mediocre from a health standpoint, and since I don't particularly need to store food for long periods of time, other dried foods like jerky aren't a huge priority. As long as I have a fridge that needs to run 24 hours a day anyway, I may as well use it for the meat and fruit I was going to dehydrate.

Indoor Electric Grills – What I'm about to point out may be common knowledge to anyone with a little common sense, but I started out as a self-taught culinary novice, so cut me some slack.

For all my fellow novices out there: my experience with using an electric grill is that it doesn't "grill" jack shit. It's basically just two frying pans stapled together, so that you can pan fry both sides of your meat at the same time. If you already own a frying pan, and you have no desire to duct tape another pan on top of it to make a kind of waffle-iron for meat, then you don't need a Foreman Grill (the brand that I tried) or any other brand of cheap indoor pseudo-grill that falls in the same category.

The Foreman Grill I bought was also kind of a pain in the ass to clean (more so than regular frying pans). This may work better with different models

I'm fairly confident in surmising that there are probably indoor grills you could buy that would actually grill your food similar to the way an outdoor grill does - the technology has to exist somewhere. But personally, I'm not willing to invest a few hundred dollars on different models to find out.

If you live in a crappy apartment with no stove, then a cheap electric grill (like the ever-popular Foreman brand I tried) would probably be nice, since you can just plug it into a wall socket and let it cook your chicken breasts while you contemplate what a dump you live in. For the rest of us who have access to exotic luxuries like stoves, it's probably not going to be helpful.

...

Like I said, the above advice is for people who are as clueless about appliances as I was (and to some degree still am) when I started learning how to cook.

There are some appliances I just haven't tried much. A lot of people, for example, make liberal use of slow cookers and pressure cookers, for example. I've never found any use for these types of appliances, so I haven't bothered trying them. Please don't be offended if you're a cooking nerd and I haven't recommended your favorite appliance – I'm sure it's lovely, I just have no use for more than two appliances, in my kitchen.

If any of the above-mentioned appliances seem like they would fit your lifestyle, obviously give them a whirl. The above warnings are just to help you make more informed decisions about what you spend your hard-earned money on. Speaking of which...

Buying Appliances

As a general rule of thumb; for any particular appliance, if you aren't buying the absolute cheapest brand on the market, you're wasting your money.

Bold statement, I know, but I remain steadfast in the face of your palpable skepticism: cheap appliances are usually the best choice for 99% of us. There are obviously some exceptions, which I'll discuss in a moment, but this rule of thumb holds true for the vast majority of appliances (and probably the vast majority of consumer-goods in general).

Allow me to explain.

Regardless of your personal preferences and health goals, the quality of your food is mostly going to be determined by a combination of A) the quality of the recipe you're working from, and B) the quality of the ingredients you're using. That's pretty much it.

The brand (and even the overall quality) of the appliances and kitchen tools you use rarely make any difference in the end product. Your steak doesn't know what kind of knife you cut it with, and regardless of whether you've got a $20 knockoff blender or a $500 Vitamix, if you make a banana-blueberry smoothie, it's going to taste like blueberries and bananas.

This applies not only to very expensive appliances, but to the mid-range appliances as well. Most people buy in the mid-range because they don't want to spend the extra money on the fancy version, but also don't want the super-cheap version that they think is going to fall apart after a week. So they buy the moderately-priced version as a kind of compromise.

This is a false distinction. In most cases, the cheap version and the mid-range version of any given appliance are pretty much identical. In some cases the two versions may literally be manufactured in the same factory in China. The extra money you pay for the mid-range model basically goes towards extra marketing and packaging costs, rather than being invested in improving the quality of the product.

Manufacturers know that people will be more likely to buy an appliance if they see it in a bunch of ads and if the packaging is shiny and pretty, so that's where they invest their money. When you buy a $40 blender, you're not buying a $40 blender; you're buying a $20 blender with an extra $10 of advertising and $10 of packaging.

Higher up on the appliance food chain, the argument for high-end appliances is that they can do things that cheap appliances can't. Occasionally this is true, but usually it's either half-true, completely untrue, or 100% true but also useless for the average customer.

With blenders, for example, the high-end blender company Blendtec likes to show off how powerful their blender is by creating publicity videos where they use their blender to grind up cell phones, broomsticks, and other crazy shit (seriously: do a search on Youtube for the phrase "Will it blend?").

This is very entertaining, but I think it's safe to say that most of us don't need a blender that can pulverize concrete, we just need one that can make smoothies. There's definitely stuff you can do with the high-power feature, like grinding your own almond flour from whole almonds, for example. But most of us can also buy almond flour at the grocery store, so the extra bells and whistles on these products often don't add much actual happiness or convenience to our lives.

If grinding your own almond flour really appeals to you for some reason, then maybe a crazy high tech nuclear-powered blender would be a great purchase for you. The same goes for all the other appliances out there that cost more than some people's cars: if you really think a microwave capable of world domination will make you happy, then go for it I guess. Just don't tell your friends how much you spent on it.

...

There are some possible exceptions to the always-buy-the-cheapest-appliance philosophy:

If you want to make weird specialty recipes, you may need weird specialty equipment.

I remember back when I was a raw foodist, there were a lot of odd recipes for things like "raw macaroni and cheese sauce", raw ice cream, etc, and you could (apparently) only be make these recipes if you had an ultra-high-powered blender. I'm sure there are other examples as well.

In my experience, there's usually a cheaper option for a lot of these specialty recipes if you're willing to do some experimentation. But if you've got a hankering for same fake mac and cheese sauce, do what you've gotta do.

If you're in some kind of situation where you need to prepare very large batches of food for a big family or something, then paying extra money for larger-sized appliances might be a good investment for your family/curling team/whatever.

If you like fancy gourmet cooking, you may want fancy gourmet appliances just for your own amusement if nothing else.

But let's be honest: if you're into fancy cooking, you bought the wrong book.

It's also worth mentioning that there are a number of cooking technologies that I've never tried before, so for all I know there could be a huge difference in quality between brands for these technologies.

For example, I've never cooked anything "sous vide", or made homemade ice cream, so maybe the premium versions of a sous vide oven or an ice cream maker are ten times better than their less expensive counterparts.

To sum up; if you're going to be buying appliances, you should never get the mid-priced version. You should be getting either the absolute cheapest version you can find, or the highest-quality version (note that "highest price" does not necessarily equal "highest quality").

The two appliances that I use every week without fail, my blender and my food processor, cost $20 and $40 respectively. Both have lasted me for years with zero replacement, zero repair, and zero problems.

The takeaway is that, when it comes to any appliance or tool in your kitchen, you should have the attitude of "guilty until proven innocent". I'm a firm believer in the idea that you can eat like royalty with nothing more than a cheap blender, a cheap food processor, and a stove.

And maybe one of those "kiss the chef" aprons.

High-Quality Ingredient Recommendations

Obviously, every ingredient you ever usin your cooking is going to vary in taste and nutritional value depending on where that ingredient comes from, how it was prepared, etc. It's a pretty common piece of advice in the cooking world that no matter how talented a cook you are, the quality of the ingredients you use are going to play a huge role in determining whether your recipes turn out amazing or just so-so.

However, in many cases this extra food-quality comes at the cost of extra hassle or extra financial expense, which can make it impractical for us to use high-quality ingredients if we're very busy, on a budget, etc.

So I'd like to take this opportunity to make some recommendations about certain specific ingredients that I use all the time which are very high-quality while simultaneously not being particularly inconvenient or expensive.

A note on taste - I don't have a particularly sensitive palette, so when I say that I can taste the difference between two versions of the same food, that means that for most people, there really is going to be a noticeable difference in taste.

If you're one of those people who, previous to becoming paleo, has destroyed the sensitivity of your taste buds with a lifetime of Funyons and Diet Coke, then hopefully this section will help you rehabilitate your battered pie hole.

...

Pepper - Fresh ground pepper tastes way better than the pre-ground pepper you buy in little bottles. If you're a lazypants like myself, "fresh ground" may sound fancy, but it doesn't take any grind to get pepper out of a grinder than it does to shake it out of a shaker - if you can turn your wrist, you can operate a pepper grinder (sorry, quadriplegics).

If you don't own one already, I recommend you buy a simple pepper grinder (a one-time $10 expense that will last you for the rest of your life), and a bottle of whole-kernel black pepper (it's right next to the regular pre-ground pepper, costs the same, and every grocery store carries it) and try it out for yourself.

Cinnamon - If you can buy fresh ground cinnamon at one of your local grocery stores, do it. I get mine from the big tubs in the spice aisle at Whole Foods, and the difference between the fresh-ground stuff and the stuff you buy pre-ground in a bottle is pretty significant.

You don't have to grind up sticks of cinnamon yourself (I've never tried it, personally), but if you want to try it that way, I bet you'd get the same effect.

Fresh cinnamon tastes amazing, so look up your local Whole Foods or hippy co-op and give it a whirl.

(Note the pattern with the above two spices: fresh-ground = noticeably tastier. Even to a muggle like myself. I don't use a very large range of spices in my cooking, so I don't know if this is true for all spices, but it's worth looking into if you dig spice)

Butter - Kerrygold is the brand of butter I recommend, hands down. It's a brand of grass-fed butter from Ireland that tastes amazing - even the unsalted kind (the only kind I use these days) tastes delicious, which isn't something I can say for other unsalted butter I've tried.

I've only experimented with a few different brands of grass-fed butter, but this one so far has been not only the best tasting, but also the most readily available (almost all grocery stores seem to carry it, even non-health-food stores).

If you look around on the web, it consistently gets high marks from foodies and professional chefs, but it's not super expensive (although it does cost more than "normal" butter).

For some reason, the Kerrygold company doesn't mention the fact that the butter is grass-fed on the product's label, but after looking into it, I found that apparently all of their products are grass-fed by default (and I believe that all of them actually come from Ireland, which is kind of neato).

The other 2 or 3 brands of unsalted grass-fed butter that I tried kind of sucked, honestly.

71

A note on grass-fed butter in general - if you're paleo, you probably already know the value of eating animal products that come from animals fed their natural diet, so I won't bore you with details about that. Grass-fed butter, however, is particularly different from grain-fed butter, because on top of having superior nutrient content, superior fatty acid profile, and so on (they way all pasture-raised animal products do), grass-fed butter actually contains something that grain-fed butter doesn't contain at all: Vitamin K2.

Vitamin K2 is a very useful nutrient for a number of different vital aspects of health (look it up, if you want), and also fairly tricky to get from other food sources. This makes grass-fed butter (regardless of brand) a fairly important thing to get into your diet if you can, just for its nutritional value (i.e. regardless of how awesome it tastes).

Health lecture over, my pretties.

Bacon - This is mostly a taste thing, but I don't screw around when it comes to bacon. I like to get big, thick slabs of the stuff from the butcher counter of the grocery store (if you ever stop by Whole Foods, try the Black Forest bacon, it's pretty pimp). I haven't had the pre-packaged kind in a long time. Bacon is honestly pretty good even when it's mediocre-quality, but why not get the good stuff?

Broccoli - I use frozen broccoli for convenience, and most frozen broccoli sucks hard. Most brands I've tried seem to be pretty much just a bag of stems with no florets, like some kind of weird broccoli-farmer practical joke.

The one brand I've found that doesn't fit this profile is the "365" brand (the generic/in-store brand at Whole Foods), which has way more florets and fewer stems. It's also pretty inexpensive.

If you'd rather buy fresh broccoli and steam it, knock yourself out. But for the sake of convenience, I only use frozen broccoli, and this is the only brand I'm willing to buy at this point.

Spinach - The opposite of a lot of other frozen veggies; I've found that for most recipes, fresh spinach is way better than the frozen or canned varieties.

If you think that you don't like spinach due to a traumatic childhood experience with canned, frozen, or cooked spinach, try making a salad or other recipe with fresh spinach leaves, and see how you like it.

Honey – I don't use honey very often, but when I do, I make it a point to use raw honey.

Raw honey, if you don't know, is just honey that hasn't been processed or pasteurized. This is a bit of a minor point in terms of health, because honey is pretty much pure sugar no matter how it's processed. But raw honey A) has some actual nutrient content, and B) typically tastes way better (in my experience), which is why I recommend it hands-down over the crap that comes in a little plastic bear.

In terms of practicality, honey is awesome because it literally never expires. Apparently, there are stories of archeologists uncovering jars of honey that were entombed in ancient Egyptian burial chambers, but despite being thousands of years old, when they examined this honey, they found that it was still edible.

Raw honey, as far as I know, is only found in health food stores. If you want to give it a whirl, be sure to try a bunch of different brands until you find one you like the taste of. The flavor varies DRASTICALLY between different brands, because bees make honey out of whatever flowering plants they can gather nectar from in the area where they live, and the plants that the bees gather nectar from can be extremely different between different regions and different honey producers.

The particular brand I'm fond of is from Y.S. Organic Bee Farms, and seems to be available at most health food stores and co-ops. It tastes so good that I could literally eat it directly out of the jar with a spoon until the fructose sent me into a sugar coma.

...

Gourmet ingredients don't have to come with gourmet price tags. If you have favorite foods, spices, or other ingredients that you use a lot, take the time and effort to do a little research and hunt around a bit, and chances are that you can find a high-quality version of that ingredient that's pretty inexpensive and makes a noticeable positive difference in your cooking.

Low-Quality Ingredient Recommendations

This section is the opposite of the previous section: here, I'd like to recommend a few ingredients for which I think it's better to buy the generic/cheaper/more convenient version, as opposed to more expensive or inconvenient versions that are supposedly "higher quality".

By the same token the benefits of these ingredients are the opposite of the ones in the previous section: buying the cheap version either A) doesn't sacrifice any quality at all, or B) makes a very small sacrifice in quality in exchange for a noticeable improvement in cost or convenience.

In no particular order:

Organic Food - As mentioned earlier in the book, I don't go out of my way to buy organic food.

Typically the foods I want are organic anyway (pasture-raised animal products, coconut oil, almond butter, etc.), so my diet is probably as much as 80%-90% organic most weeks whether I want it to be or not.

But with certain foods, I deliberately avoid the organic version in favor of the significantly-lower-priced, non-organic version. I do this because, to put it simply, the health benefits of organic food are somewhat speculative, but the extra cost of organic food is decidedly non-speculative.

For example, are organic cookies better than non-organic cookies? Quite possibly: maybe the organic ones will prevent some potentially harmful chemicals from entering your body, reduce the amount of pollution in the world, or any of a number of other things. But in practical terms, the sugar in the cookies is bad for you regardless of how much pesticide was used in growing the sugarcane, and the pollution from the truck that carried those cookies to the store is the same regardless of whether the truck's cargo is organic or not. So in this case, I probably wouldn't spend the extra money.

Note that this is just one example (and most of us paleo-nerds probably aren't going to be buying cookies anyway).

For another (possibly more relevant) example from my own eating habits: I never buy organic berries. I buy big bags of frozen, non-organic berries at ordinary non-health-food stores, and they are *way* less expensive than any type of organic berry (fresh or frozen).

When I do this, I may be sacrificing some nutrient content or something as far as I know. But I'm confident in assuming that for the most part, blueberries are going to end up being pretty damn healthy any way you slice it.

Coconut Oil - I use a fair amount of coconut oil, so I buy the generic Whole Foods brand (the

"365" brand), which is typically about 40%-50% less expensive than other brands. There's no discernible reduction in any of the standard quality indicators: the 365 brand is organic, "extra virgin", etc. It also tastes the same as other coconut oils as far as I can tell.

Note that with coconut oil, it actually is important to buy it organic and "virgin", because these terms describe genuine differences in processing methods that have a measurable impact on the nutrient content of the final product (unlike a lot of organic foods, where the difference between organic and non-organic is often just a matter of which brand of pesticide was used).

Also note that there's no difference between the terms "virgin" and "extra virgin"- they mean the same thing when it comes to coconut oil. Companies just use the phrase "extra virgin" to sound extra fancy.

The 365 brand is both organic and virgin, and costs significantly less than any other brand I've found, so that's the one I you use.

Frozen Produce - As mentioned in the "Basic Principles" section, not only do I highly recommend frozen ingredients in general, but I'm particularly partial to frozen produce. It's worth mentioning again in this section, because the frozen version of any particular fruit or vegetable is often less expensive than the "fresh" version, with no sacrifice in quality whatsoever (go back and read that section again if you need a reminder why).

Sweet Potato Fries - Also on the topic of frozen foods - I often buy pre-made frozen sweet potato fries.   The brand I typically get is called Alexia, and they come in a bag in the freezer section of most grocery stores.

These pre-made fries contain some non-ideal ingredients (I believe they're fried in canola oil or something similar), which is unfortunate.   But the actual content of the food itself is 99% sweet potato, so I'm not too worried about the remaining 1% of oil and seasoning.

Unless you're trying to lose weight (in which case you should probably be avoiding all tubers, no matter what form they come in), these are lovely tasting, very convenient (since they're pre-made and frozen), last forever (frozen), very useful to eat post-workout for replenishing muscle glycogen, and fairly inexpensive.

Mayonnaise - A lot of the time, if a recipe calls for mayo, I just use actual mayo, rather than going to the trouble of making paleo mayo out of coconut/olive oil.

If I was ever planning on eating tons of the stuff, I would probably go to the extra trouble of making the paleo version, but since I prefer to use light mayo whenever a dish calls for it, I doubt that a few ounces of dairy mayo, spread out over 4-5 days, will impact my health much.

I've experimented with making paleo mayo (there are a number of good recipes for that out on the internet, if you're interested), and I found that buying a jar of good-quality mayo (ideally without too much seed oil) is usually more convenient, and possibly less expensive when you factor in the cost of the paleo-mayo ingredients.

Neither regular mayo nor the paleo version makes me feel noticeably better or worse when I consume them.

If you love globbing on huge amounts of mayo with certain dishes, it's probably a good idea to put in a little extra work and make the healthy stuff, but if you're like me and don't use much of it, you may want to save yourself the trouble.

Almond/Coconut Milk - I like to buy cartons of flavored almond milk and/or coconut milk (primarily to use as the liquid base in smoothies and shakes), rather than grinding my own almond milk from scratch or buying "pure" canned coconut milk.

The additives and flavoring in these slightly-processed milks are definitely not healthy, but there's only a small amount of added sweetener, and I only drink about a cup every other day or so. It wouldn't be a good idea to drink several cups of this stuff per day, but in the context of a diet that is as healthy as mine, I'm not at all concerned about such a small amount of artificial flavoring.

Additionally, I think smoothies have a tendency to taste somewhat bland if you don't add a little sweetener to them, and since smoothies are one of the ways that I get nutrient-dense berries and green vegetables into my diet, I'm willing to make this small compromise to enjoy my food more.

With these convenience and taste benefits taken into account, I find these somewhat-processed milks to be a very useful alternative to the liquids that are commonly recommended for shakes and smoothies (like dairy or fruit juice), since the almond and coconut milks retain a lot of the

81

nutrient content of the almonds/coconuts, and come with a much smaller amount of sugar/lactose.

I do use completely unflavored canned coconut milk on a regular basis, alternating it with the more processed/flavored stuff. And just to be extra careful about my sugar consumption, I only use the sweetened variety on workout days.

There's a quick tip on finding inexpensive canned coconut milk in the section entitled "A Few Miscellaneous Tricks".

If you want a brand recommendation, the brand of sweetened coconut milk that I'm currently using is the annoyingly titled "So Delicious" brand. I'm sure any brand will do as long as it isn't loaded up with high fructose corn syrup and dead baby tears.

Spinach - I like to buy those big plastic boxes of spinach, just because they're pre-washed and pre-dried, and I go through a lot of spinach.

This saves me some time in washing and drying the spinach leaves, and since the spinach in these plastic is so thoroughly dried (presumably by some kind of fancy spinach-drying machine), it lasts a bit longer in the fridge than regular spinach that I wash myself.

...

There are potentially quite a few little shortcuts like the ones detailed above that can help you shave some extra moeny off of your grocery bill and some time off of your weekly food preparation, (without sacrificing quality). This, as usual, will be determined by your individual preferences and circumstances, so be sure to experiment with the foods you like and see if you can find "shortcuts".

Keep in mind that taking shortcuts isn't the same as cutting corners. If you can do something that isn't technically paleo, and still feel strong, alert, and full of energy, then you're doing something right. Be strategically lazy, not lazy-lazy.

A Few Miscellaneous Tricks

Here are a few little culinary tricks that I personally get a lot of mileage out of, but that I haven't seen mentioned elsewhere in the paleo community. They're all completely unrelated to each other, and none of them will revolutionize your life, but it's taken me a while to collect all of these little tidbits, and I find them extremely helpful.

In no particular order...

...

To find out what the actual shelf-life is for any food, I use www.StillTasty.com.

This site allows you to type in the name of a food (i.e. "eggs"), click on the sub-category that most closely matches what you've got (i.e. "eggs – fresh, raw, in the shell"), and then see a breakdown of how long it will last in different circumstances (i.e. 3-5 weeks in the fridge, 1 year in the freezer).

Each entry also usually contains a few tips on storage and handling for that specific food (such as "do not freeze eggs in their shell") to make your life easier.

This site has frequently saved me money by preventing me from throwing out food that I mistakenly thought might be expired, and has also occasionally saved me from using recently-expired ingredients by accident. It's completely free, easy to use, and highly recommended.

...

As a way to both save myself some money and increase the amount of healthy fats in my diet, whenever I cook meat I try to reincorporate the liquid fat that melts off the meat back into the recipe I'm making, rather than pouring it down the drain

You'll notice that in a lot of the recipes in this book, I mention this as a step in the recipe, and this is because I do this pretty much whenever I make anything involving meat.

This is partially a money-saving strategy, because this liquid fat that melts off is part of the meat that you paid good money for, so when yo udo this, you're getting more calories-per-pound-of-meat than someone who pours the fat down the drain.

You're also increasing the amount of healthy, natural fat content in whatever dish you're preparing, making it more nutrient-rich and satiating.

It's a win-win.

The only limitation is that this strategy only works with certain types of recipes, For example, if you're cooking a steak, you obviously can't inject the liquid fat back into the steak. Typically "mixed" recipes work best for this (i.e. recipes made with ingredients that have been ground/diced/chopped and then mixed together). For examples, see this book's recipes for Paleo Mashed Potatoes, Hamburger Salad, and Bacon Brussels Sprout Slaw, among others. This type of mixed, textured dish can usually "absorb" the liquid fat fairly easily, since the fat coats the mixed ingredients (similar to the way salad dressing coats salad).

If you're cooking meat to be used in a dish where you can't mix the fat back in (such as when you cook bacon for bacon-and-eggs), you can still save the fat in a jar for later use, either as a cooking oil to coat your frying pan, or to mix in with a future recipe.

Two tips if you're planning on saving the fat for later. First, you'll want to run the liquid fat through a strainer before storing it in order to filter out all the little crispy bits of burned meat (which can go bad during storage). Second, even though rendered fat has a very long shelf life even at room temperature, I like to store it in my fridge anyway, just to be on the safe side.

...

I've noticed that in my area, Asian markets and grocery stores sell canned coconut milk way cheaper than both health-food stores and "regular" grocery stores.

I can only speculate about why this is, but I assume it's an economy-of-scale thing. Since a lot of Asian dishes use coconut milk, a store catering to Asian-style foods and cooking can bulk-order coconut milk at lower prices.

Or something. Whatever the reason is, I just take my cheap coconut milk and don't ask questions.

You may have to try a few different brands of coconut milk to find one that is low-priced but still good-quality (I've found that some brands are more watery than others).

The little Asian grocery store that I go to also has pretty cheap produce for certain types of food (their avocados, for example, are surprisingly inexpensive). So when you go looking for coconut milk, be sure to poke around the rest of the store too.

The only (hypothetical) drawback to this is that none of the food in these stores is organic. I've explained my thoughts on organic food elsewhere in this book, but if you're a stickler for eating only 100% organic food, you're out of luck.

Other than that, Asian grocery stores are great, and I highly recommend you search out any that may be in your area (I had to go through several before I found one that I liked, so be sure to check out as many as you can).

...

Having a stockpile of eggs on hand is very helpful. They last 3-5 weeks in the fridge, can be prepared in a bunch of different ways, are very satiating, and can be cooked up in about 5 minutes. Also, if your eggs are well-sourced, they're extremely nutrient-dense and good for you. They're pretty much the ultimate convenience food, and also a great back-up option to keep on hand in case you run out of other foods or just want to whip up something simple.

...

If you're restricting your carbohydrates for fat loss purposes, and you get a sweet-craving, I've found that mixing unflavored Greek yogurt with some flavored protein powder is an excellent antidote. I use a chocolate-flavored protein powder, and the final product is like a kind of low-rent chocolate mousse.

The artificial flavoring in the protein powder isn't ideal from a health standpoint, and the yogurt (i.e. dairy) isn't ideal from a fat loss standpoint. But the "damage" is pretty minimal: the whey protein and healthy fat is very useful for your body, the Greek yogurt contains some probiotics, and most importantly, this will completely satisfy your sweet tooth without the use of any kind of sugar.

For those of you who have trouble digesting dairy, I'll point out that I'm fairly sensitive to dairy myself, and for some reason the Greek yogurt doesn't particularly disagree with me (probably because it's fermented).

Overall, it's a very effective compromise.

If you're insistent on not eating even the smallest amount of processed food (or dairy, for that matter), I've also found that a very small amount of almond butter and raw honey, mixed in a bowl and eaten directly with a spoon, tastes shockingly good given that it's just two ingredients.

The ratio of almond butter to honey should be about 2:1, and the overall amount should be kept very small to avoid interfering too much with your weight loss – literally about half a tablespoon of raw honey and one tablespoon of almond butter. Since the amounts are so little, you'll just be eating small eighth-of-a-teaspoon-sized bites at a time, but because of how rich and flavorful this combo is, it's surprisingly satisfying.

...

As you may know, cultivating helpful digestive bacteria is extremely important for many different aspects of health. Personally, however, I found it a little tricky to implement back when I first started experimenting with it.

Based on the general principle that whole foods are usually more complete and overall healthier than processed foods and supplements, I wanted to get my probiotics from whole-food sources, rather than from little bacteria pills.

The only two sources I'm aware of for whole-food probiotics are dirt and fermented foods. For obvious reasons, I chose fermented foods. Unfortunately, I found out that there was a little problem with fermented foods: in my humble opinion, they taste horrible.

The process of fermenting food pretty much universally creates a sour taste that is pretty unpleasant, and personally I had some difficulty getting around this. I'm generally pretty tolerant of gulping down crappy-tasting food for health purposes, but the first time I tried sauerkraut I hated it so much it made my teeth hurt. Some people apparently like the taste of sauerkraut, but, surprisingly, partially-rotted sour-tasting-cabbage-slurry doesn't appeal to all of us.

I also tried unsuccessfully to locate other kinds of fermented foods (like natto and tempeh) to see if they tasted any better. Unfortunately I couldn't find these foods in my area, and didn't want to go through the trouble of making and fermenting them myself from scratch.

I'm happy to say that eventually, I found two solutions to this problem, both of which have made this particular aspect of my diet extremely easy to handle.

The first is kombucha. If you're never heard of it, kombucha is basically a type of fermented tea. It tastes pretty mediocre, but A) it's not gag-inducing, and B) because it's a liquid, it's easy to chug down quickly, minimizng the sour taste even further. The taste isn't at all bad – the unflavored kombucha that I drink tastes kind of like a very tart apple juice, but without the sweetness.

There are a number of different brands of kombucha on the market, and apparently some are sweetened with sugar, which I would assume kind of cancels out the health benefits. I believe there are also varieties that are pasteurized, which by definition is probably going to kill off the bacteria you're trying to get, unless they add probiotics back in after the pasteurization process.

The kombucha I buy is completely unflavored and also "raw" (i.e. unpasteurized), and despite this lack of tampering, it tastes fine.

It's also easy to find – all the local co-ops and Whole Foods stores in my area seem to carry this stuff. It's a little on the pricy side - one bottle, which holds about 3 cups, generally costs about $3 a bottle. But since you'll only be drinking it periodically, the cost is minimal. Although it's a whole food, I treat it like a supplement; rather than sipping on it like a normal drink, I typically gulp down a cup (as in, one measuring cup) about 3 times per week. Overall, it's a really easy habit to maintain.

If you don't like kombucha or want something that's a bit cheaper per-ounce, I've found that kefir can fill pretty much the same role (i.e. the fact that it's a liquid makes it easy to gulp down a cup and minimize the sour taste).

Kefir, if you don't know, is basically liquid yogurt – sort of a thick, sour-ish milk. The fact that it's dairy is not going to be ideal for a lot of people (those who are dairy-sensitive, trying to lose weight, and so on), but the fact that it's fermented may make it more agreeable than regular dairy, so you can try it if you want and see how your body responds. Personally, I prefer kombucha.

The other food I find helpful is Greek yogurt mixed with a sweetener of some kind. I covered a version of this in the previous section, but there are some variations I'll mention here.

Greek yogurt tastes pretty mediocre by itself, but mixing it with other ingredients for flavor (like, fruit or honey, or the aforementioned protein powder) makes it really tasty, like a dessert. I'm particularly fond of Greek yogurt, raw honey, and almond butter.

If you're eating for weight loss, want to increase your protein intake, or just trying to avoid sugar in general, the flavored protein powder option would probably be up your alley. It's a bit less healthy (because it's processed and contains artificial sweeteners), but still very viable, and it will allow you to keep your sugar/carbohydrates low and give yourself an extra protein boost if those things are of interest to you.

From what I understand, the scientific literature on the subject indicates that artificial sweetener (like the sucralose found in most protein powders) will probably have some degree of negative impact on stomach bacteria. But in this case, since the yogurt contains probiotics, worst-case scenario is that the probiotics and artificial sweeteners cancel each other out. Best case scenario, we're taking two steps forward and one step back (which is still one step forward) with our overall stomach bacteria levels. Which is fine by me if I get to eat something that tastes like chocolate.

If you don't have a problem with using whole-food flavoring ingredients that contain some sugar, like fruit or honey, this won't even be an issue for you.

Adding kombucha and Greek yogurt to my diet has made it extremely easy and painless for me to take care of this whole "helpful bacteria" aspect of my health. If you're like me, and don't want to deal with artificial supplements or the gag-inducing taste of other fermented foods, I highly recommend these foods. Go to hell sauerkraut!

...

So, those are my sneaky little tricks. A fairly rag-tag collection, I'm sure you'll agree. But it took me a quite a bit of time, effort, and experimentation to come up with them, and they do come in handy. I use a lot of these tricks on an almost daily basis, so hopefully you'll find a few that you like and get as much use out of them as I do.

Part 2:

A Selection of
Practical Recipes Suitable
for Lazy, Hedonistic
Cavepersons

An Introduction
to the Recipes

The following recipes have all been taken directly from my own personal diet and eating habits. I've personally tried all of them out, tested them, and adapted them where necessary.

None of these recipes where included in the book because I just read about them on the internet; and thought they sounded promising. The only reason why the following recipes made the cut is because I use them all on a regular basis.

You don't need a bunch of random paleo recipes from me; you can get hundreds of those on the internet if you'd like to wade through them all. The recipes in this book have all been included for the following reasons:

1) As illustrations of the basic principles outlined earlier in the book. All of these recipes are conducive to batching or long-term storage, they're healthy and full of nutritional variety, they're relatively easy to prepare, and they taste awesome.
2) So that anyone who wants to start experimenting with the concepts in this book (or who is just new to cooking in

general) has a convenient place to get started, without hunting through all the time-consuming, impractical recipes on the internet to find the small handful of practical ones.

3) So that you know what I eat on a daily basis, if you're curious. I have two little folders on my computer related to food. One is labeled "recipes", and consists of all the recipes that I've come across that I haven't tried yet but want to experiment with. The other is labeled "keepers", and consists of all the recipes I've tried out for myself, made a number of times, and found to be both delicious and practical. This section is prety much a collection of my "keeper" file.

I've tried to make the descriptions of these recipes as detailed and beginner-friendly as possible, so that people who suck at cooking will be able to make these recipes just as easily as more experienced foodies. Hopefully readers of this book who are already good at cooking will also find the extra details helpful, rather than patronizing or tedious.

I've also included a little "notes" section with each recipe, which details miscellaneous bits of advice that I think might be useful, such as recipe variations, cooking tips, storage advice, recommended brands or ingredients, etc.

When I'm not eating out, these recipes comprise about 95% of my the food I eat on a dailiy basis, so I hope you like them as much as I do, or at least find them useful as a starting point for your own culinary experiments.

Bacon Brussels
Sprout Slaw

This is one of my staples. Although Brussels-sprout-based recipes are not exactly popular, this one doesn't particularly seem to taste like Brussels sprouts, so if you don't normally like the taste of them you're good to go. This recipe is a slightly modified version of one that I initially read on www.foodrenegade.com, which was actually a guest post by the author of www.lifeasaplate.com. I recommend both sites if you're into gourmet, non-lazy cooking (although this particular recipe is lazy-friendly).

Ingredients

4 cups shredded Brussels sprouts
1 pound bacon
1 small-medium red onion
¾ cup beef or chicken stock
1 tbsp dijon mustard
1 tbsp Maple syrup
½ cup slivered or sliced almonds
1-3 tbsp butter

Directions

- Cook the bacon in a pan to your desired crispiness (I like mine somewhat soft). Pour the leftover liquid bacon fat into a large saucepan. Set the bacon aside to cool.
- Heat the saucepan (with the liquid bacon fat) on medium heat and let it warm up while you do the following steps. Be sure to keep the saucepan covered, so the soon-to-be-sizzling bacon fat doesn't splatter on you.
- Wash the Brussels sprouts and cut off the little stems at the base of each one.
- Put the sprouts into a food processor and shred them. If you don't have a food processor, you can probably get away with just chopping them up by hand.
- Dice the onion to whatever size chunks you prefer. I like mine diced fairly small.
- The bacon fat in the saucepan should be sizzling by now. Add the chopped onion to it and let it cook until it's lightly browned (usually just a minute or two).
- When the onion is cooked to your liking, add the shredded sprouts, beef or chicken stock, maple syrup, and Dijon mustard.
- Cook 5-7 minutes, stirring constantly until the liquid is absorbed and the sprouts are soft.
- Dump everything into a big bowl. While it's still hot, put a few pads of butter onto it and mix it in so that the butter melts and coats the whole mixture.

-   Dice the bacon. I cut mine into pieces about the size of a postage stamp.
-   Mix the diced bacon and sliced almonds into the mixture. Serve hot.

Notes

-   I do all of the vegetable prep while the bacon is cooking (I typically have to do several "batches" of bacon, since a pound of bacon doesn't fit in a normal-sized pan). So I don't do the above steps separately, I'm usually doing a number of them simultaneously.
-   The local Whole Foods that I shop at sells a particular brand of chicken stock ("Pacific Natural Foods Organic Free Range Chicken Broth") that comes in 4-packs, which each little package containing 8 oz of chicken stock. They look kind of like little juice boxes, but with chicken stock. These small single-serving packages are convenient for this recipe, because you only need a small amount of stock for this recipe at any given time.
-   I've found that when I buy fresh Brussels sprouts, the little mesh bag they come in contains the perfect amount for this recipe, so I typically don't measure out 4 cups, I just use whatever is in the bag.
-   If you want, this dish also tastes great with dried cranberries (you can mix them in, at the end, along with the bacon and almonds). The adds a nice sweet note to this mostly-

savory dish, but I've found that it's also really tasty without them, and leaving the cranberries out makes the dish sugarless. If you want to experiment with adding them, I've found that ½ cup - 1 cup works well.

Hamburger Salad

This is a (very slightly) modified version of a recipe from www.theclothesmakethegirl.com. I find it very efficient as a way of getting both more grass-fed beef into my diet in a way that's convenient and inexpensive.

Ingredients

ground beef (any quantity – it doesn't affect the rest of the recipe)
several cups fresh spinach (I don't measure this, I just throw handfuls in until it feels like a good mix)
salt
black pepper
olive oil
raspberry blush vinegar
mayo
Italian herb mix (any will do – see notes)

Directions

 - Season the ground beef with salt, pepper, and garlic powder to taste (I recommend being fairly liberal with the garlic powder and pepper, and more moderate with the salt). Brown the beef in a frying pan, and when it's cooked, set it aside to cool (save the liquid beef fat from the pan, if you'd like to reincorporate it back into the dish)

– When the beef has cooled, crumble it up and mix it with as much shredded spinach as you like (I recommend adding a little at a time, shredding the spinach with your hands as you go, until you feel like you've got a good balance)

– Sprinkle with Italian herb mix (to taste – I like being fairly liberal with this as well), and stir thoroughly.

– Mix the liquid beef fat into the mixture if you'd like.

– Whenever your ready to eat, put some of the dish in a bowl and mix in a small dollop of mayo, a splash of olive oil, a splash of raspberry blush vinegar, and more black pepper (all of this to taste, obviously). Mix well and serve hot.

Notes

– The Italian herb mix I use is a pre-made one that I get at Whole Foods (in one of those big self-serve tubs in the spice section). You can make your own Italian-style mix from separate spices if you want, but I've never bothered.

- Sorry I can't give you more specific ingredient amounts for this recipe, but since it's mostly just ground beef and seasoning, the vast majority of it really is "to taste".
- The mayo in this recipe can easily be substituted for a non-dairy paleo version – I've had it both ways, and they both taste great.

Cherry Chicken Salad

Here's a dirt-simple one that I'm quite fond of. If I'm going somewhere and I want to be a nerd and bring a plastic container of my own food with me, this is one of my go-to options, because it tastes best when it's served cold or at room temperature.

Ingredients

x number of chicken breasts (see note below; I typically use 4-5)
mayo
½ cup - 1 cup dried cherries (dried cranberries are also great)

Directions

- pan fry the chicken breasts
- let the chicken cool, then dice it or shred it
- add mayo to taste
- mix in the cherries
- serve cold

- I've found that preparing one chicken breast for every day's-worth of food I'm making is a good rule of thumb (i.e. if I'm making 4 days of food, I use 4 chicken breasts). This will obviously vary based on whether you plan to eat more than one serving of this recipe per day, but that's the rule of thumb I use.
- I currently prefer to use dried cherries in this recipe, but if you're counting your pennies, dried cranberries cost about half as much per pound where I live.
- Adding some extra garnish to this recipe (like crushed walnuts, for example) is definitely a possibility.
- This can also be made into A) a salad, by just dumping it on a bed of greens, or B) a kind of chicken salad sandwich, by wrapping it in a large lettuce leaf.

Bacon Cheeseburger

I'm a huge fan of traditional bacon cheeseburgers - this is basically that minus the bun. It barely qualifies as a recipe, but I decided to list it in recipe-format for clarity. It's simple and hedonistic, just the way I like it.

<u>Ingredients</u>

about ½ lb bacon
3 lbs ground beef
cheese (see notes)
ketchup

optional: whatever toppings you like on regular burgers

<u>Directions</u>

– Cook the bacon, and either dice it, or cut it into hamburger-sized slices (I prefer dicing it).

- Divide the ground beef into 6 portions (each will be about ½ lb) and shape each portion into patties. Cook these.
- If you're storing these ingredients for later, store them separately.
- Whenever you're ready to eat, assemble the bacon on top of one of the burger patties and heat it up in the micowave.
- When hot, top the burger with cheese and heat a little more, so that the cheese melts.
- Top it with whatever sauce or sauces you like (ketchup, mustard, mayo, bbq sauce, etc.), and heat it a little more if these sauces are cold.
- Pick the whole big greasy mess up with your bare hands and eat it. Be prepared to have juices running down all over your hands and face in glorious rivulets.

Notes

- this is one of those recipes that I would prefer to cook fresh every time I eat it, but since this would require cooking both the bacon and the hamburger, it's a bit too time-consuming for me, so I just batch it all ahead of time. You might want to experiment with partial-batching for a nice, fresh-cooked burger if you have the time.
- The cheese I use is a raw mild cheddar. If you're not into raw dairy (or dairy in general) do your own thing.
- If you'd like some kind of bun-like thing to hold this together, as usual, a couple lettuce

leaves will work. It will probably still be messy as hell.

- I've found guacamole to be an excellent topping for this. You can even smush some alfalfa sprouts into the guac for added texture, if you want to go extra fancy.

- If you're only going to eat one of these a day, making 6 patties may be a little much (6 days is kind of a while for the cooked ingredients to sit in the fridge). I usually eat 1-2 per day, so it's not a problem for me.

- Without a bun that you can use to squeeze everything together, you're probably somewhat limited as far as the number of toppings you can fit onto this thing. If you're one of those people that really likes to pile the toppings on, you'll have to experiment to see how much you can get away with before the whole thing becomes structurally unsound.

- Some people apparently use things like sliced jicama (or other paleo-approved vegetables) to approximate french fries. I've never tried it, but if you're jonesing for the burger-and-fries experience, you may want to investigate this. If you're athletically active and/or don't have any need to lose weight, regular french fries or sweet potato fries will probably be fine (that's how I do it).

Amazing Fake
Mashed Potatoes

This is one of the latest recipes that I've experimented with, and I'm in love with it to the point of creepiness.

Depending on how fundamentalist you are about paleo "rules", you may be anti-potato. As I wrote about earlier in the book, I'm completely open to eating starchy tubers, including regular potatoes, but I like having other options as well, so this is nice for that.

Note that I've developed the ingredient amounts around my own tastes (bacon, chives, lots of butter, etc.), so you may have to adapt the numbers significantly.

This is easy to make, super tasty, keeps well, has very little carbohydrate and zero sugar (if you're eating for fat loss), contains healthy doses of a fairly nutrient-dense vegetable (cauliflower), and has a substantial dose of healthy fats as well. I'm pretty smitten with it.

Ingredients

2 heads of cauliflower
8 cloves garlic
6-8 tablespoons butter (I like to go heavy-butter)
½ - ¾ lb bacon
scallions to taste

Directions

- Fill a saucepan about halfway with water and bring to a boil
- Chop up however much of the chives you want, crush the garlic in a garlic press, and break apart the cauliflower florets into pieces.
- When the water is boiling, add the cauliflower and put the cover on the saucepan. Boil for 7-8 minutes. When it's done boiling, set it aside to cool.
- Fry the bacon until it's fairly crispy and dice it into small pieces. Use the still-hot bacon pan to briefly saute the crushed garlic (1-2 minutes only). Set aside.
- Put the boiled cauliflower in a food processor and process it until it's pretty well ground-up.
- Add the butter and garlic, process again until the consistency is smooth and creamy.
- Scoop this newly formed mashed-potato-like mixture out of the food processor into a bowl, and mix in the diced bacon and chives. Serve hot.

Notes

- I actually have to make this dish in two separate batches; neither my saucepan nor my food processor are large enough to hold more than one head of cauliflower at a time.
- I really like garlic, so I use a fair amount in this recipe. Obviously lower the amount of garlic if you want ... and don't eat this before going on a date.

Raw Chocolate Mousse

This recipe is actually something I learned how to make back when I was a raw foodist. Variations on this recipe are pretty popular among the raw food crowd, but I don't think I've ever seen something like this in the paleo community (probably because, it can be fairly high in sugar depending on how much honey you use).

For this reason, I would put this dish more in the realm of "semi-healthy indulgence", rather than making it a cornerstone of your diet, but it is damn good, and way healthier than most chocolate-based dishes.

Ingredients

2 avocados
1 tsp vanilla extract
½ cup cacao powder
½ cup pitted dates
raw honey to taste

Directions

- Soak the dates for at least 30 minutes until they're soft.
- Peel and pit the avocados, and throw them into a food processor along with the dates. Blend until the mixture becomes a smooth paste (don't stop until the dates are fully blended with the avocado, otherwise the mixture will turn out a little chunky).
- Add the cacao powder, honey, and vanilla, and blend until the mixture is smooth and well-mixed. Can be served at room temperature or chilled.

Notes

- You can technically make this in a blender, but it's an enormous pain in the ass. If you don't have a food processor, I would either skip this recipe, or just go get one already (see Appliances section).
- The texture of the final product is actually more like a pudding than a mousse, in my opinion, but all the raw food chefs refer to this as a mousse. Just thought I'd warn you, in case you make this recipe and exclaim, "May the gods damn this Sean Robertson fellow to the deepest bowels of hell...this is clearly a pudding, not a mousse!"
- If you want you can use almost anything with a creamy texture to either partially or completely replace the avocado (some

118

variations on this recipe have involved bananas and nut butters, for example). Personally I think the mild taste and smooth texture of avocados provides the best base for this recipe, but you can try a half-and-half avocado/banana or avocado/nut butter mixture if you want to experiment.

–   Serving this to friends and family as regular chocolate pudding, and then revealing that it was made out of avocados, is kind of fun.

–   By themselves, avocados spoil somewhat quickly. But for some reason, even though this recipe is mostly avocado, it lasts significantly longer in the fridge than whole avocados by themselves.

–   I recommend using a cacao powder that is as minimally processed as possible, and that is 100% cacao with no other ingredients. We're mixing in other ingredients with this recipe, so it won't taste bitter at all, and it will help keep the additive-content down.

–   You can add as much cacao as you want to kick up the chocolate flavor, but be conservative with the honey, since it's very sugary.

–   On a related note, most raw chocolate mousse recipes call for agave nectar, which is very popular in the raw food community as a "natural sweetener". As you may know, agave nectar actually fairly processed, and often contains more fructose than high fructose corn syrup. Avoid it.

Disembodied Taco Meat

Most paleo taco/burrito recipes involve some kind of tortilla substitute to hold the meat in. I've experimented with making a kind of imitation tortilla out of egg whites, wrapping the taco meat in lettuce leaves, etc. So far, none of these have particularly impressed me. So these days, I just eat the taco meat by itself with a spoon or fork, straight out of the bowl, which massively simplifies things and still tastes damn good.

The following recipe is going to seem kind of ghetto because of how simple it is, but if you give it a try I think you'll find it very serviceable.

Ingredients

3 lbs ground turkey
1-2 packets taco seasoning (depending on how much seasoning each packet contains)
guacamole

optional: 1-2 cans black beans

Directions

- Brown the ground turkey in a saucepan.
- Add taco seasoning and stir for a few more minutes.
- Serve with a few dollops of guacamole.

Notes

- Depending on how you feel about beans/legumes, if you'd like you can add a can of black beans right before you add the taco seasoning, and it adds some nice texture to the recipe. One can of beans spread out over several meals isn't a big deal for most of us, so give it a try if you like Mexican dishes.
- I use prepackaged taco seasoning that comes in a little packet. If you aren't as lazy as me, it's fairly easy to buy the necessary spices and combine them into your own homemade taco seasoning if you're so inclined.
- As additional proof of my epic laziness, I often buy my guacamole pre-made. I've experimented with making it myself, but Whole Foods sells small tubs of it that they make in-store, and I've found that this tastes just as good. Guac is pretty easy to make yourself though if you're not as tragically lazy as me.
- When making a big batch of this to eat throughout the week, I recommend storing the guac separately from the taco meat, and

just mixing it in each time you heat up a bowl.

- If you want to mix things up a little, you can eat this on a bed of lettuce like a salad, or wrap it in a lettuce leaf as an improvised tortilla.
- If you want to jazz it up further, add in whatever else you normally like on tacos (salsa, some cheese if you're a dairy-eater, etc).

Edible Guacamole

This recipe is based on a guacamole recipe from www.lifeasaplate.com. I call this "edible" guacamole because the addition of the bacon makes it good enough that I sometimes eat it straight-up with a spoon, rather than using it as a topping or dip like normal guac. It can obviously be used like regular guac as well – when I'm not using a pre-made guacamole, I frequently use this as the guacamole for the previous recipe (Disembodied Taco Meat), and it can be used for almost any dish that calls for regular guacamole.

Ingredients

4 avocados
4 tomatoes
1 lb bacon
¼ diced onion
2 tbsp unflavored Greek yogurt
2 tbsp mayo
2 tbsp lime juice

Directions

- Cook the bacon however you'd like (I recommend fairly crispy for this recipe) and dice it. Save the liquid bacon fat in a bowl for later.
- Peel and pit the avocados, throw them in a food processor, and blend into a smooth paste.
- Throw in the yogurt, mayo, and lime juice and blend again until smooth. Pour/scrape into a large bowl.
- Dice the tomato and onion (I recommend chopping the onion relatively small and the tomato chunky).
- Mix the diced onion, tomato, and bacon into the avocado mixture, along with the liquid bacon fat, and mix well.

Notes

- Adding the liquid bacon fat back into the guac will make the recipe a bit more liquidy at room temperature – it will re-harden when you chill it in the fridge, but if you want to avoid this, you can leave the bacon fat out and save it for some other use.
- Additionally, depending on how mushy your avocados are, you may want to cut down on the amount of mayo, yogurt, or even lime juice you add, since these will affect the consistency as well.

No-Fake-Flour
Paleo Pancakes

There are quite a few recipes floating around for paleo pancakes, and they all differ quite a bit in their in the ingredients they use. The only downside to most of these pancake (and other baked-good) recipes is that they use imitation flours like almond flour or coconut flour. There's nothing particularly wrong with these ingredients, but personally I've noticed that for some reason they don't make me feel particularly energetic after I eat them. I can't account for this scientifically, because almonds and coconuts are pretty nutritious when eaten in their whole-food form, but whatever the cause, the affects are noticeable.

Fortunately, this recipe uses no fake flour (hence the name), which for me is a big selling point. It contains relatively few ingredients, is easy to make, and tastes awesome. I like these so much that I can literally eat them by themselves with no toppings (which is more than I can say even for "real" pancakes) – however, there are a bunch of options for toppings discussed in the Notes section.

Ingredients

2 eggs
½ cup almond butter
½ cup unsweetened apple sauce
¼ tsp vanilla extract
¼ tsp cinnamon
coconut oil

Directions

- Mix all of the ingredients (except the coconut oil) in a bowl. Softening the almond butter in the microwave may be helpful if it's cold.
- Heat a frying pan over medium heat and coat with coconut oil (I like using a small pan to keep the size of the pancakes more manageable).
- Pour a dollop of the batter onto the pan (amount of batter = however big you want your pancake to end up). Since the mixture is a little thicker than traditional pancake batter, you'll probably have to jiggle the pan a bit to get the batter to settle into a flat pancake shape.
- Fry the pancake carefully for a few minutes until it solidifies. For me it typically takes 2-3 minutes, but watch it carefully - if you try flipping it before it's ready it will break apart, and if you wait too long it can burn fairly easy. A good way of testing this is to jiggle the pan, and if the pancake is ready, it will actually slide around the pan a bit (as

opposed to just jiggling if it's not fully solid yet).

- When the batter has solidified, flip the pancake over to toast the other side (this typically takes less time than the first side).
- Slide onto a plate and repeat the procedure until you've used up all your batter. Serve hot.

Notes

- Other types of nut butters besides almond butter will probably work just as well for for this, so use whatever your favorite is.
- Although these taste surprisingly good by themselves, there are obviously lots of things you can top them with. If you're not too worried about sugar in your diet, a good-quality maple syrup is the obvious choice, but they're also excellent topped with almost any kind of fruit (blueberries, diced apple, and banana slices are all damn good). Other options include butter, apple sauce, and various jams/jellies.
- Unlike regular pancakes, I find that these are pretty suitable for batching and storing in the fridge. Sometimes I take them straight out of the fridge and eat them cold, without heating them up or putting any toppings on them. Don't judge me.

Orange Chicken

My staple recipes for sneaking more greens into my diet are both bacon-based; the Bacon Brussels Sprout Slaw and the Bacon Broccoli Salad (detailed elsewhere). However, if you're not as into bacon as I am, this is an easy, tasty, and batch-friendly alternative.

Ingredients

3 chicken breasts
4 tbsp coconut oil
1 bag frozen broccoli
juice from 2 medium oranges
1 tbsp soy sauce
2 tbsp minced garlic

Directions

- Heat the broccoli in a microwave and set aside.
- Heat a large saucepan over medium heat.
- When saucepan is hot, add the coconut oil and let it heat up for a second.

- When the oil is hot, add the chicken and cook it until it's just barely done, stirring frequently.
- Once the chicken is cooked, add the orange juice, soy sauce, and garlic, and stir until all the ingredients are well mixed
- Let the mixture sit, and when the liquid comes to a light boil, lower the heat to medium-low. Allow it to bubble for 3-4 more minutes.
- Turn the heat off and mix in the broccoli. Serve hot.

Notes

- This recipe would probably work with beef and possibly some other meats as well, but I haven't tried other meats yet. If you're a fan of beef, by all means use that instead.
- I would recommend that you drain off the excess liquid before storing this in the fridge, to prevent the mixture from getting too goopy during storage.

Fat Mixture

Alright, this recipe probably isn't going to sound appetizing. And in all fairness, it's going to end up looking pretty ugly as well.

But beauty is only skin deep, and this recipe is actually pretty good if you make it right. More importantly, it has a few very nice benefits from a convenience standpoint;

It literally never spoils, even when it's left sitting out at room temperature for a month.

It's dirt-simple to make, and perfect for large-scale batching.

It's surprisingly filling, so you don't need much of it to make a simple meal.

And it's very portable, so you can bring it with you and eat it anywhere.

All of these advantages will hopefully outweigh the fact that it looks pretty ghetto.

The idea for this came from a number of different sources. It started when I first heard about pemmican, a traditional food made out of fat and dried meat (if you've never heard of it, look it up, it's interesting). Pemmican is a little impractical to make, and fairly expensive to buy pre-mad, so I crossed it off my list as a potential convenience food.

However, I remained fascinated by the fact that properly-made pemmican pretty much never spoils. So I set about experimenting to create my own non-pemmican mixture of unspoilable ingredients.

The following "recipe" is the result. It's basically just a bunch of healthy fats that happen to be completely non-perishable, mixed with some miscellaneous long-shelf-life ingredients for flavor, which is whey I refer to as simply as a "fat mixture".

Despite how unappetizing that sounds, I recommend you give it a try and experiment with making your own version of this little oddity (it's extremely easy to experiment with since there's no cooking involved). If you try a few variations of this and find one that you like, you'll have a dish that pound-for-pound is pretty much the ultimate convenience food.

See the notes section for all the options I've experimented with, including an explanation of why I use each ingredient, and treat the following recipe like a basic template.

Ingredients

1 cup coconut oil
¼ – ½ cup ghee, depending on your taste preferences (see notes if you don't know what ghee is)
⅛ - ¼ cup raw honey (see notes for dosing recommendation)
½ - 1 cup almonds
½ - 1 cup walnuts

(optional) a small amount of dried fruit (I like dried cherries)

(optional) various flavoring ingredients (see notes)

Directions

- Unless it's fairly warm where you live, the coconut oil and ghee will be solid at room temperature, so heat them lightly in the microwave to melt them into their liquid form.
- When the ghee and coconut oil are in their liquid or semi-liquid state, combine them and the honey in a big bowl and stir until they're well-mixed.
- Grind the almonds and walnuts in a food processor (see notes if you don't have a food processor). Grind them into a powder if you want the final dish to be somewhat smooth, or leave them chunky if you prefer.
- Pour the ground-up nut mixture into the liquid fat mixture to form a super-mixture of fattyness.
- Add whatever dried fruit and/or flavoring ingredients you're using (if any), and mix well.
- Pour the mixture into a storage container, and put it in the fridge to solidify.
- Once the mixture has solidified, it can usually be stored at room temperature (see notes), but you can leave it in the fridge if you want. Whenever you're ready to eat,

just take a spoon and eat it straight out of the container.

Notes

- This recipe is great for travel and "on-the-go" type situations, because (as mentioned) you can eat it straight out of the container with a spoon; no heating, mixing, preparing, etc. The only caveat is that if you're going to be taking it somewhere fairly hot, it might melt a bit. The fact that it's easy to make, easy to batch, and never spoils still makes it an attractive option to keep around the house, even if you live someplace hot and have to keep it in the fridge to keep it solid.
- If it's cold where you live, you might have to soften up the honey a little before mixing it in with the liquid fats.
- If you don't have a food processor to grind the nuts up, then A) you haven't been listening to my advice about how you should get one, damn your eyes, and B) just buy walnuts (since walnuts are fairly soft) and crush them yourself via your favorite method.
- Here are the explanations for why I personally use the ingredients in the above recipe:
  - Coconut oil is the well-known in the paleo community for being ridiculously healthy, it never goes bad, and it tastes excellent.

- Ghee (if you don't know what it is) is a type of clarified butter that never spoils. I'm not a big fan of the taste, but it's useful as a healthy, natural fat, that never spoils, and it adds some nutritional variety to the mix. Be careful with amounts, because too much can overpower the taste of the other ingredients.
- Raw honey is delicious and also never spoils (I'm sure you're seeing a pattern here). It's used here only as a flavoring agent: I recommend using the absolute minimum amount possible, since honey is basically pure sugar. The dish doesn't taste very good unflavored though, so include at least a little. If you want to minimize sugar in your diet as much as possible, you can leave the honey out at your own risk and see if you like the taste.
- Nuts are perishable to some degree, but they have a very long shelf life, so I include them here for flavor, texture, and nutritional variety. The reason why I use almonds and walnuts in particular is just because they contain some nutrients I'm interested in including in my diet – if you like the taste of other nuts, use those.
- Optional flavoring:
  - There are potentially a pretty wide range of flavoring agents you can add to this recipe; anything powdered or liquid that doesn't spoil is fair game. I've only tried

a limited number of things, so use your imagination.

- Dried fruit is mediocre from a health standpoint, but small amounts improve the taste of this recipe a lot, in my opinion. I think cherries complement the others flavors best.
- The two flavorings that I personally use all the time are cinnamon and cacao powder. You could use these individually, but they go great together.
- Back when I was experimenting with artificial sweeteners, I tried putting some in this dish as a substitute for the honey, and it turned out pretty gross, so I don't recommend you go that route.
- Coconut shavings work well, but aren't necessary since the coconut oil adds a lot of coconut flavor already. They do add some extra texture though, which is nice.

Coconut Chicken

This recipe is fun, and also a bit of a mess to make. For that reason, I don't make it as often as other chicken-based recipes in this book, but I really enjoy it as an occasional change of pace from my usual staples.

Ingredients

4 chicken breasts
½ cup shredded coconut
½ cup almond flour
¼ tsp salt
1 egg
coconut oil

Directions

- Mix shredded coconut, almond flour, and salt in a bowl.
- Beat the egg in another bowl .
- Take one chicken breast and dip it in the egg bowl, making sure that the egg evenly coats the surface of the chicken.

- Roll the chicken breast around in the coconut/almond flour until it's thoroughly coated in the dry mixture.
- Repeat with each chicken breast.
- Heat a frying pan over medium-high heat, coat with coconut oil when hot, and pan fry like a normal chicken breast. Serve hot.

Notes

- I find these tasty enough to eat without any sauce or anything. But if you're open to a little extra sugar, this goes great with a fruit-based dipping sauce, as well as things like mango salsa, various kinds of fruit chutney, etc.

Green Smoothie Example

The phenomenon of the "green smoothie" is common among certain types of healthy-eating enthusiasts (I was first introduced to the concept when I was a raw foodist).

At heart, it's a simple concept: since leafy green vegetables are extremely healthy but also very bland tasting, one method for avoiding the bland taste is to throw some leafy greens into a fruit smoothie. The sweet taste of the fruit masks the bland or bitter taste of the greens, and the blending process also grinds up the tough, fibrous greens so that they're essentially pre-chewed for you and you can just drink them down.

The reason I include this particular smoothie recipe is not because it's a special recipe, but just to demonstrate the green smoothie concept if you haven't tried it. Smoothies are very easy to be creative with, so you can use this as an example to start with if you want to do your own diabolical smoothie experimentation (see the notes section for my own extensive list of smoothie tips).

Ingredients

(keep in mind that the following amounts are fairly approximate)

About half a cup each of frozen blueberries, strawberries, and cherries
1 cup fresh spinach
1-2 cups coconut milk

Directions

- Thaw/defrost the berries a little to soften them up for blending. If you want a super-cold smoothie (and your blender is strong enough) you can leave them completely frozen.
- Blend the berries and coconut milk until smooth (you can add the berries a little at a time, or use extra coconut milk, if it helps your blender work better).
- Add the spinach, blend until smooth again. Serve cold.

Notes

- Use the highest setting on your blender, and let it blend for as long as it needs to in order to fully grind up the fiber from the berries and spinach, otherwise your smoothie may be a little chunky.
- Note that the color of a green smoothie is not necessarily green; the "green" part refers to the fact that you're mixing in green vegetables (you sneaky dog).

- The reason I use spinach is because it contains tons of useful nutrients, has a very mild taste that is barely noticeable in most smoothies, and isn't very fibrous, so it blends up very easily and unobtrusively.
- I like using berries in my smoothies because they taste good and are apparently very nutrient-dense. I also like that I can buy big bags of frozen berries relatively inexpensively, and they last forever in the freezer.
- If you'd like to experiment with different combinations of fruit/vegetables/liquid, here are some guidelines I discovered back when I was making lots of smoothies:
    - Oranges are a shitty choice for a green smoothie, because the pulp doesn't get blended up very well.
    - Bananas are considered somewhat inferior by the paleo community (I believe the standard rationale is that they're higher in sugar or something), but the flavor of bananas is very versatile for pairing with other fruits, and the creamy texture is great for smoothies.
    - You're usually going to want to mix multiple kinds of fruits together when making smoothies, rather than using just one kind, in order to make the taste more interesting.
    - You don't have to use green vegetables for your smoothies, but greens are tend to be the most nutrient-dense vegetables

and the ones that we could all use more of in our diets.

- Kale, in my experience, tastes horrible, and the bitterness is strong enough to overpower the sweetness of the other ingredients.

- Some vegetables are too fibrous for a smoothie (at least when they're raw), and just won't get ground up very well unless you've got a really high-powered blender. I've found that kale, cabbage, and celery, for example, are all too tough to make a smoothie out of. You also probably couldn't grind up cruciferous vegetables like broccoli and Brussels sprouts, but I've never tried.

- A smoothie with a thick texture (such as one with bananas in it) will help grind up the vegetables better than a thinner smoothie.

- Whole cream makes a delicious liquid base for smoothies – if you tolerate dairy well, use it.

- If you aren't using frozen fruit, you can throw in a few ice cubes to make your smoothie cold.

- I would avoid using fruit juice as a liquid base, because (as you're no doubt aware) it's just a step or two away from sugar water, and you've already got whole fruit in the smoothie anyway.

- You can also experiment with more elaborate combinations. For example, banana smoothies tend to go well with

144

things like nut butters and cacao powder.
- Due to the slightly higher sugar content of this smoothie (flavored coconut milk + fruit) compared to a lot of paleo foods, people trying to lose weight should probably partake sparingly.

Green Protein Shake

The inspiration for this recipe came from a shake that Tim Ferriss mentions in his book "The 4 Hour Body". I like drinking it after weight lifting because it contains a little bit of everything that's good for muscles: a modicum of protein, some carbohydrate for replenishing muscle glycogen, and some healthy coconut fat and nutrient-rich spinach for overall health. It also serves a similar function as a green smoothie, in that it allows me to get some greens into my diet without chewing on salad all day.

Ingredients

1 cup flavored coconut milk
2 raw eggs
2 tbsp almond butter
1 cup fresh spinach
½ tsp cinnamon

optional: ½-1 tsp vanilla extract

Directions

-   Toss everything in a blender and blend until smooth, paying particular attention to make sure the spinach is fully ground and the consistency of the shake is non-chunky.

Notes

-   If it's hot outside and you want to cool off, blend in some ice cubes
-   The reason why spinach is used in this recipe (as opposed to any other leafy green) is because it's very mild tasting and not very fibrous, which makes it barely-noticeable when blended thoroughly into the shake.
-   Since I use pasture-raised eggs, I have no worries about salmonella. Also, from what I understand, even shitty factory-farmed eggs aren't as big of a salmonella risk as most people think, as long as they're refrigerated. That being said, go at your own risk and don't sue me if something weird happens. Personally, I eat two raw eggs per day (in the form of shakes and smoothies like this one), 4-6 days per week, and I've never had any problems. Your mileage may vary.

Asian Marinated Chicken

This is actually a recipe that I found on an online Atkins Diet discussion forum, which I came across while searching for low-carbohydrate recipes online. The Atkins Diet is not a source I would usually go to for healthy recipes, but this particular one is 95% paleo (the other 5% being a single packet of Splenda, which is probably optional anyway).

When I'm making some kind of marinaded chicken breast recipe, I usually prefer the Thai Peanut Chicken recipe detailed earlier. But this recipe makes for a nice change of pace, and is equally easy to prepare.

Ingredients

4 chicken breasts
½ cup soy sauce
¼ cup water
About an inch-long piece of ginger
1 tsp onion powder
2 cloves garlic
1 packet Splenda (or any sweetener, equivalent to about 2 tsp sugar)
1 tsp sesame oil

Directions

- Peel the ginger and garlic and chop into tiny pieces.
- Mix all the ingredients together in whatever storage container you want to use to marinate your chicken.
- Place the chicken in the liquid and allow to marinate overnight.
- When ready to eat, pan fry or grill chicken and serve hot.

Notes

- Normally I avoid artificial sweeteners as much as possible, but one packet of Splenda spread out over 4 chicken breasts is pretty minimal, especially when you consider the fact that it's a marinade (rather than a sauce or something - the marinade just gets drained off anyway). If you want to experiment a little, I'm sure you could substitute some honey or another "natural" sweetener.
- Just like the Thai Peanut Chicken, I like to partial-batch this recipe.
- This marinade would probably be good with other kinds of meat as well (beef in particular seems like it would be a good fit), but so far I've only used it with chicken.

Guacamole Deviled Eggs

This little recipe is a variation of a variation - it's based on a recipe by Tamara Baysinger, which I read on marksdailyapple.com, which is itself a variation of the classic deviled egg recipe (substituting guacamole for mayo). I find it surprisingly filling, and it's also a great recipe if you want to include more eggs in your diet, but find eggs prepared the normal way (scrambled, over easy, etc.) to be too boring.

Ingredients

- eggs
- guacamole
- lime juice
- thinly sliced ham

Directions

- Hard boil as many eggs as you want.
- When you're ready to eat, take however many of the hard-boiled eggs eggs you want and cut them in half. Scoop the yolks out

into a bowl (be careful not to damage the whites, since they're going to be the receptacle for the other ingredients).

- Mix the yolks with some lime juice (I use about ¼ tsp per egg) and a little bit of guacamole (I use about a 1:1 ratio of egg yolk to guacamole).
- Scoop the mixture back into the hollowed-out egg whites.
- Top with thin slices of ham. Serve at room temperature or chilled.

Notes

- This is one of the few recipes in the book that is suitable not only for private consumption, but also makes for snazzy finger food for dinner parties, social gatherings, etc. If you're serving it to friends, you may want to pay more attention to the "presentation". Other than that, the recipe stays the same regardless of whether you're the host of a fancy party or just a bachelor eating over the sink.
- The classic (mayo-based) deviled eggs recipe has a lot of variations with added ingredients, including paprika, hot sauce, ground dry mustard, white wine vinegar, etc. So there's lots of room for personalization with this recipe.
- The ham I use is just thinly sliced ham from the deli counter.

Chicken and Egg Salad

This is a nice alternative to the "Cherry Chicken Salad" detailed earlier, specifically because it doesn't contain any dried fruit, which A) I'm not always in the mood for, and B) I know a lot of people prefer to avoid. It's also a nice dish to eat chilled when it's hot outside.

Ingredients

3-4 chicken breasts
4-8 eggs hard-boiled eggs (depending on how eggy you want the final product to be)
Approximately 1 tbsp white wine vinegar (depending on the amount of mayo you use)
1 cup diced celery
mayo to taste
Old Bay seasoning to taste

(optional) diced onion to taste

<u>Directions</u>

- Pan fry or grill chicken breasts and dice them into small chunks
- Dice the hard-boiled eggs as well, and mix the egg and chicken in a large bowl.
- In a separate bowl, mix the mayo and white wine vinegar, then pour over the chicken and eggs.
- Add the diced celery, onion (if using), and Old Bay seasoning and mix thoroughly. Serve chilled.

<u>Notes</u>

- If you want to store this for any length of time, it's typically best to store the vinegar/mayo sauce separately to keep the dish relatively dry and prevent spoilage.
- If you really like the taste of mayo, you can skip the vinegar altogether and just use extra mayo.

Ground Beef
Sweet Potato Curry

This is a variation o a recipe I found on http://inthenightlife.wordpress.com. The presence of sweet potato is nice for post-workout recovery (although there's only a small amount in this recipe – mostly I just love sweet potatoes).

<u>Ingredients</u>

2 lbs ground beef
1 medium sweet potato
1 tbsp coconut oil
2 tbsp fresh ginger
2 tbsp red curry paste
2 tbs curry powder
1 can full-fat coconut milk

<u>Directions</u>

- Dice the sweet potato into small chunks (whatever size you'd prefer to have in your curry – I like mine about ½ an inch square).
- Brown the ground beef and set aside (save the liquid fat from the pan for later).

- Mince the garlic and ginger.
- Heat a saucepan over medium heat, and coat the pan with coconut oil.
- Add the garlic, curry paste, and curry powder to the pan, and saute for about a minute, so that the spices are lightly toasted.
- Add the coconut milk, sweet potato, ground beef, and the liquid beef fat that you saved, and stir until the ingredients are well mixed Break up the ground beef into small chunks while doing this.
- Cover and simmer over low heat until the sweet potato is cooked through (about 30 minutes). Serve hot.

Notes

- If you want, you can throw in some shredded coconut just before serving, which adds some extra texture and a little more coconut flavor.

Paleo Cereal

There are a number of paleo recipes for grain-free paleo versions of cereal/oatmeal online. After some experimentation, the following is what I personally use.

Ingredients

Slivered almonds
Shredded coconut
Coconut milk
Blueberries

Directions

- Mix all of the above ingredients together, in whatever amounts you prefer. Then eat them.

Notes

- As mentioned elsewhere in this book, I use a store-bought, somewhat-processed, sweetened coconut milk. If you want to save yourself from the horrible fate that I've consigned myself to, you can use unflavored coconut milk, but the recipe will probably end up tasting a little more bland unless you sweeten it with a little honey (or whatever sweetener you prefer).

- I often have this with almond milk instead of coconut milk (also a sweetened, store-bought version), and that tastes great as well.

- If you'd like to make the flavor a little more complex, you can use a variety of berries (instead of just blueberries), and a variety of nuts (instead of just almonds). You can also add seeds (sunflower or pumpkin seeds would probably work well), for either taste or nutritional variety.

- If you want to spice it up a little, you can also toss in a few crushed pieces of dark chocolate, some cinnamon, etc. This is one of those recipes that's easy to modify and experiment with, since there's no cooking or baking involved.

- Although it's really easy to throw this together on the spot whenever the mood strikes, if you want to eat this every day, you can mix together a huge tub of all the dry ingredients at the beginning of the week, and then whenever you want just pour out a bowl, add the milk and berries, and rock and roll.

- Although I love using coconut/almond milk for this recipe, whole cream or half-and-half are both delicious with this, if you tolerate dairy.

Paleo Oatmeal

This recipe was adapted from one found on www.marksdailyapple.com. I don't eat it very often when the weather is warm, but during cold months it's an awesome comfort food. Also, if you used to be an oatmeal fan before eliminating grain from your diet, this actually tastes pretty damn similar to real oatmeal, and it's great for anyone who is having trouble adjusting to grain-free breakfasts.

Since I typically just whip up one bowl of this at a time whenever the mood strikes (rather than batching it and eating it for a week straight), I'll start by describing how I make one (fairly large) bowl. See the notes section for tips on batching if you're so inclined.

Ingredients

one handful of walnuts
one handful of pecans
½ tsp ground cinnamon
1/8 tsp ground ginger
1/8 tsp nutmeg
1 tbsp almond butter

1 banana
3 eggs
¼ cup coconut milk

Directions

- Throw the walnuts and pecans in a food processor and grind them down until they're mostly powdered (don't grind them all the way into a powder, leave them a little coarse), and set aside.
- Mash the banana and set aside.
- Mix the eggs, coconut milk, and almond butter in a bowl (if you've been keeping the almond butter in the fridge, warm it up a little so it's easier to mix).
- When the mixture is well-combined, mix in the mashed banana.
- Finally, mix in the ground nuts and the spices, and stir well.
- Heat the mixture in the microwave in 20-30 second bursts so that it warms gradually. Stir the mixture in between each burst to prevent the eggs from solidifying, and continue the process until the oatmeal has reached your desired consistency/warmth. Serve hot.

Notes

- I normally prefer fresh ginger for any recipe that calls for it, but for this one, you'll have to use powdered ginger. Most powdered ginger sucks, so try to get fresh-ground ginger if possible (I get mine from a co-op, where it's sold in tubs in the spice section). You'll know it's fresh-ground if you open up the tub and it still has that awesome lemony smell that a freshly cut piece of ginger has.

– If you don't like using microwaves because you think it's going to mutate your food or something, I'm sure you could warm this up on your stove if you wanted to.

– To partial-batch this recipe, take the measurements for the walnuts and pecans listed above (i.e. the amonut for a single serving of this recipe), and multiply that by however many days'-worth of this recipe you want to prepare in advance. Measure out the appropriate amount of nuts, mix them and grind them up, and then store the resulting nut mixture. With the nuts pre-ground (and thus, no food processor to clean), it's pretty easy to make a bowl of this whenever you want.

Turkey Roll-Ups

This dish doesn't make a full meal, but it's great as a snack. You can also cut these up into little pieces and serve them on toothpicks as finger food, if you're into throwing dinner parties. Either way, these are tasty.

Ingredients

Thin slices of deli turkey
Mayonnaise
Sundried tomatoes (the kind that come in a jar with oil)
Watercress
Black pepper

Directions

- Wash and de-stem the watercress.
- If the sundried tomatoes aren't already chopped, chop a small amount and mix with a little mayo.
- Lay a slice of turkey on a plate and spread the tomato-mayo mixture over it.

163

- Grind pepper over the mixture to taste, and top with a bunch of watercress leaves.
- Roll the turkey slice up into a gooey cylinder and enjoy.

Notes

- If the turkey slices you're using are thin and fragile, you may want to use two turkey slices per roll to prevent the turkey from breaking and spilling the contents all over the place. Not that that's ever happened to me...
- When first making these, go easy on the mayo and tomato – the flavors are strong, so it's easy to overdo these ingredients and make something that tastes like a mouthful of tomato-y mayonnaise. A little experimentation will allow you to determine how much of these ingredients to use so that they complement that turkey and watercress.
- If you don't like watercress or can't get it at your local grocery store, fresh spinach leaves also work well.

Trail Mix Example

By paleo standards, this is a pretty borderline food – it contains more sugar and PUFA's than the average paleo nerd like myself would prefer, but it also has some decent nutrient content, and none of the ingredients are too problematic.

With that in mind, trail mix is tasty, convenient, portable, and doesn't expire, making it very attractive as a snack food.

It's also very easy to experiment with by swapping different ingredients in and out, so it can be customized to any individual's taste or mood at the drop of a hat.

Consider the following recipe a basic template to experiment with.

Ingredients

½ cup almonds
½ cup walnuts
½ cup sunflower seeds
1 tbsp coconut oil
½ - 1 tsp cinnamon
1 tbsp vanilla extract

1 tsp salt

A little raw honey to taste (just enough to sweeten it a little)

Dried fruit to taste (just enough to add a little extra flavor – I like dried cherries or apricots, or if I'm feeling feisty, a little of both)

Directions

- Combine the coconut oil, vanilla, and honey in a bowl (if necessary, soften up the coconut oil and honey in the microwave).
- Mix the nuts, seeds, and dried fruit in a big bowl.
- Pour the bowl of liquid ingredients over the bowl of dry ingredients, and stir until the dry ingredients are coated completely in the liquid ingredients.
- Sprinkle the cinnamon over everything and mix again, then allow everything to dry.

Notes

- Some people apparently like baking their trail mix, but I've never tried this. Give it a whirl if you want.
- Most trail mix recipes are based around dry ingredients, but I'm very partial to adding a little bit of liquid (preferably something sticky, like coconut oil or honey) and some spices, in order to give the trail mix a nice coating. The coating makes it a little messy to eat, so you might want to reconfigure this

recipe so all the ingredients are dry if you'd like to avoid this.

- I personally like the salty/sweet combo, but you can easily ditch the salt if you're avoiding it for health reasons, or if you just don't like the taste.
- Additional ideas for ingredients to add:
  - shredded coconut
  - dark chocolate pieces (use sparingly)
  - different nuts (pecans, macadamia nuts, etc.)
  - different kinds of dried fruit (almost any kind will work)
  - extra spices (depending on what combo you end up with, you can even make a spicy/savory trail mix)

Roast Beef

When I make roast beef, I cook a big hunk of it, keep it in the fridge, and cut off slices of it throughout the week. I find it tasty enough on its own that I don't garnish it or put sauce on it or anything like that, and it's pretty fun to spend one of my daily meals just chewing on hunks of meat.

Ingredients

3 to 3 1/2 lbs of boneless rump roast
Olive oil
8 slivers of garlic (usually ends up being 2-3 cloves)
Salt
Black pepper

Directions

– Start with the roast at room temperature (if you've been storing it in the fridge, take it out about an hour before cooking). Preheat the oven to 375°F.

- Make 8 small incisions around the roast with a knife. Place a sliver of garlic into each incision.
- Take a tablespoon or so of olive oil and spread it all around the roast, and sprinkle the roast with salt and pepper.
- Place the roast directly on an oven rack, with a drip pan on the rack below it to catch the juices.
- Brown the roast at 375°F for half an hour, then lower the heat to 225°F. The roast should take 2-3 more hours to cook at this point. When the roast just starts to drip its juices, and is brown on the outside, it should be good to go.
- When the roast is done cooking, remove the garlic slivers. Store the meat as a whole slab (i.e. don't cut it up into portions) in order to keep the juices in. Cut off slices throughout the week, and serve hot.

Notes

- If the roast has a fatty side, you can place that side facing up while it cooks, so that as the fat melts it will bathe the roast in its juices. Neato.
- Moniter the roast carefully towards the end of the 2-3 hour cooking window. I've found that it's pretty easy to overcook, and having to throw away a week's worth of meat because it's tough and unchewable is extremely lame.

Sauteed Greens
with Mustard Sauce

This is one of the few instances in which I actually eat greens on their own (rather than mixing them in with something tastier like bacon). It's also one of the only non-batchable recipes in this book, but it's quick and easy to make and very healthy. Not a meal unto itself, but makes a great side dish.

Ingredients

Spinach
Snow peas
Brown mustard
Butter
Paprika
Black pepper

Directions

- Heat a frying pan over medium heat, and melt a large pad of butter in the pan (be

171

generous with the butter; it's going to coat your vegetables).

- Toss a small handful of snow peas onto the pan and let them cook for a minute or two while you mix up the sauce.
- To make the sauce, put 1 tbsp butter in a small bowl and melt it in the microwave.
- When the butter is melted, mix in 1 tbsp brown mustard, a little water (about ½ tbsp), and pepper and paprika to taste.
- Now that the snow peas have had 2-3 minutes to cook, throw a big handful of spinach into the pan and pour the sauce over it.
- Stir the vegetables and sauce around, ensuring that the vegetables are evenly coated, until the spinach starts to wilt (which will happen fairly quickly).
- Remove from pan and serve hot.

Notes

- I often eat this with eggs (hard boiled or over easy, usually), because for some reason this combination seems to work well together.
- There's a lot of room to experiment with adding stuff to the sauce. I like the above sauce mixture for both its taste and simplicity, but you could easily experiment with adding more spices, thickening it with some dairy, etc.

- The snow-pea-and-spinach combo also tastes very good with just a thick coating of butter and no sauce, so if I'm in the mood for something different, I'll frequently do that.

Fancy-Pants Omelet

Alright, in the big scheme of things this probably isn't that fancy, but it's damn good, and one of the few non-batchable foods that I eat no a regular basis

And compared to the ghetto one-ingredient omelets I tried making in college, this is pretty fancy.

Although you'll technically be making this "from scratch" each time, it's still pretty quick to make, and many of the ingredients can be prepared ahead of time (partial batching – see notes).

Ingredients

3-4 Eggs
Cheese (see notes)
1 small tomato
¼ to ½ an onion
Bacon to taste (pre-cooked, see notes)
Butter
Salt
Black pepper

<u>Directions</u>

- Grate however much cheese you want onto a plate, dice the tomato and onion, and whisk the eggs.
- Heat a frying pan on medium heat, and add a big ol' pad of butter to coat the pan.
- Saute the diced onion in the butter (add more butter if you have to). If you're using pre-cooked bacon that's been in the fridge, toss the bacon in as well to heat it up.
- When the onion is lightly browned, dump it and the bacon onto a plate and return the frying pan to medium heat. The pan should still be well-greased from the previous steps - if it's not, add a little more butter to re-grease it.
- Pour the eggs into the frying pan. Use whatever omelet-making technique you prefer to solidify the omelet (I prefer the scraping method). If you don't know how to make an omelet, look up a few methods online and pick your favorite.
- Just as the eggs are starting to solidify, but while they're still a little moist, spread the diced tomato, onion, cheese, and bacon over half of the omelet.
- Sprinkle salt and pepper over the whole arrangement, then cover it with a lid and let it cook another 1-2 minutes (enough for the cheese to melt and the eggs to finish solidifying). Be careful not to let it go to long or you'll burn the omelet.

176

- Slide the omelet off onto a plate and flip it closed.

Notes

- For cheese, I usually use a raw mild cheddar. If you're not into raw dairy, use whatever cheese you prefer, preferably a cheddar or good-quality Parmesan. If you're one of those people who is hardcore about not using dairy, this would probably still be a bitchin' omelet without the cheese..
- If I'm planning on making this omelet every day in a given week, I just buy whatever amounts of the ingredients I'll need for 4-5 of these (one per day for 4-5 days).
- I cook the bacon in advance, dice it into little chunks, and keep it in the fridge, sprinkling on as much as I feel like using for each omelet.
- Having all of the ingredients ready-to-go makes the preparation for this omelet pretty fast and easy. The bacon is prepared as mentioned above, and if you really want, you could pre-dice the onion and pre-grate the cheese into plastic containers (don't pre-dice the tomato).
- Keep in mind that tomatoes are one of those foods that varies drastically in quality, and tomato-based dishes live or die by the quality of the tomatoes you use. Be sure to use firm, fresh tomatoes for this dish.

Stand-Alone Meatballs

Enterprising paleo cooks would probably eat these meatballs with spaghetti squash, homemade pasta sauce, etc, in order to approximate normal spaghetti-and-meatballs. Personally I prefer to just eat these straight-up, without sauce or anything else, and they're actually very tasty this way. This is also one of my favorite ways of getting more grass-fed beef in my diet.

Ingredients

2 lbs ground beef
1 lb Italian sausage (if you have a choice between spicy and mild, I recommend spicy)
1 tbsp Italian seasoning
1 tsp onion powder
1 tsp garlic powder
1 tsp cayenne pepper
1 tsp black pepper
Coconut oil (to coat your frying pan)

Directions

- Knead the sausage and ground beef together with your hands until well-combined.
- Mix the spices together in a bowl.
- Squish the meat flat and sprinkle the spice mixture over it, then fold the spices into the meat and knead it some more until the spices have been thoroughly incorporated into the meat.
- Break the meat up into little balls, about an inch and a half in diameter.
- Heat a frying pan over medium heat and coat with coconut oil.
- Place the meatballs on the pan and cook them. When the underside is browned, flip the meatballs over and cook the other side (just like making little hamburger patties).
- Serve hot. For bonus points, eat these with your fingers, like little meat bonbons.

Notes

- I'm not a fan of baking or slow-cooking meatballs, but if you prefer one of those methods, I'm sure it wouldn't affect the basic recipe or ingredients.
- In order to make it easier to flip the meatballs during the cooking process, and to prevent the meatballs from rolling around, I like to ever-so-slightly flatten them before

placing them in the pan. Which technically makes each meatball more of a meat-spheroid, I suppose. I'm not changing the title though.

Bacon Broccoli Salad

This recipe is surprisingly tasty given how dirt-simple it is. If you want a version that is even tastier (but more elaborate and not as suitable for storage), see the notes section.

Ingredients

1 pound of bacon
1 ½ bags of frozen broccoli
Mayo to taste

Directions

- Cook the bacon to your desired crispiness (I like mine fairly soft). Save the liquid bacon fat.
- Defrost the broccoli in the microwave.
- Dice the bacon into fairly small pieces, and mix it in with the broccoli.
- Pour the liquid bacon fat over the bacon and broccoli and mix, so that the mixture is coated in bacon fat.

- When you're ready to eat, mix in mayo to taste (I like to keep it fairly light). Can be served hot or chilled.

Notes

- Don't store this recipe with the mayo already mixed in; the extra moisture will reduce the dish's shelf life.
- This recipe was inspired by a fairly different recipe that I found on paleodietlifestyle.com, under the name "Bacon, Grape, and Broccoli Salad". This recipe had way more ingredients and tasted awesome when it was fresh, but unfortunately didn't keep well in the fridge in my experience (mostly because it used fresh grapes, which decay pretty quickly). If you'd like a tastier but more high-maintenance option (for when you want to entertain guests or something), check that recipe out.
- Two ingredients that also work well with this dish are chopped onion and slivered almonds. Depending on what I'm in the mood for, I often use one or both of these to change up the taste, and the almonds add a nice crunchy texture as well.

Thai Peanut Chicken

This one has become a staple of my diet lately, due to the fact that it's very simple but very flavorful. This is currently my favorite way of preparing chicken breasts.

Ingredients

4 chicken breasts
½ cup peanut butter (doesn't matter if it's creamy or crunchy; I use creamy personally)
¼ – ½ cup honey
¼ cup soy sauce
1 tbsp curry powder
2 cloves garlic
About an inch-long piece of fresh ginger
1 tsp sesame oil

Instructions

– Peel the ginger and garlic. Chop them up as finely as possibly and set aside.

185

- Mix the peanut butter, honey, soy sauce, and sesame oil until smooth.
- Stir in the curry powder, ginger, and garlic and mix well.
- Take about a third of this mixture and coat the bottom of a plastic container. Place the chicken in the container and dump the rest of the marinade over it. Spread the marinade around, making sure that the entire surface of each chicken breast is coated.
- Marinate the chicken in the fridge overnight.
- When ready to eat, rinse all of the marinade off the chicken, grill or pan fry, and serve hot.

Notes

- Peanuts are on the paleo watch-list, but since you're rinsing the marinade off before cooking, you're not actually consuming any of the peanut butter (other than any trace amount that works its way into the chicken flesh). Even if you're normally very anti-peanut, you can still enjoy this recipe without angering the paleo gods.
- I strongly prefer partial-batching this recipe (allowing the meat to sit and marinate in the fridge and cooking individual chicken breasts as needed).
- A lot of recipes for Thai-style peanut chicken involve a peanut dipping sauce for the chicken. I don't use any sauce personally,

because I find the marinaded chicken has a very nice flavor on its own, and this allows me to avoid consuming the extra peanuts, sugar, and other non-ideal ingredients that are in most peanut sauces.

Appendix 1:
Recipes Conducive to Fat Loss

As mentioned previously, at the time of this writing I'm currently experimenting with reducing my body fat for athletic purposes. I won't bore you with the details of my exact regimen, because frankly I'm still experimenting with various strategies myself. However, since a lot of people who are into healthy eating are also interested in weight loss, I'll specify which of the recipes in this book would fit the criteria of good weight loss foods according to standard paleo thinking.

The criteria I'm using is that a recipe good fat loss recipe is A) low in overall carbohydrates, B) little or no sugar content (including fructose from fruit), even if it does contain some carbohydrate, and C) little or no dairy (other than butter, which is mostly fat).

These 3 criteria are definitely not the only factors that affect fat loss; these are just convenient criteria for a book targeted at the paleo community, since a lot of paleo dieters focus on reducing carbohydrates, and particularly various sugars (including fructose and lactose) as a method for fat loss. Other factors (exercise, digestive bacteria, sex hormone levels, etc.) are outside the scope of this book.

Note that I don't necessarily agree with what the paleo community considers an effective fat loss diet. This section is just a convenient appendix for any readers of this book who want to reduce their carbohydrate intake.

With that in mind, here's a short list of the recipes in this book that I think will be of interest to most paleo dieters, including page numbers and brief notes where relevant.

- Amazing Fake Mashed Potatoes, p. 113
- Asian Marinated Chicken, p. 149
- Bacon Broccoli Salad (contains a little dairy in the form of mayonnaise, which can be substituted for any type of paleo mayonnaise if desired), p. 183
- Bacon Cheeseburger (small amount of dairy in the form of cheese, can be omitted or modified), p. 109
- Chicken and Egg Salad (contains a little mayo, can be substituted), p. 153
- Disembodied Taco meat (negligible amount of carbohydrate in the guacamole, depending on how much you use), p. 121
- Fancy-Pants Omelet (contains a little dairy in the form of cheese), p. 175
- Guacamole Deviled Eggs (negligible amount of carbohydrate in the guacamole, depending on how much you use), p. 151
- Hamburger Salad (contains a little mayo, can be substituted), p. 103

- Orange Chicken (the orange juice is just a marinade, so any trace amounts of fructose in the meat shouldn't be an issue), p. 131
- Roast Beef, p. 169
- Sauteed Greens with Mustard Sauce, p. 171
- Stand-Alone Meatballs, p. 179
- Thai Peanut Chicken (the honey and peanut butter is just a marinade, and shouldn't affect the carbohydrate level of the dish much, if at all), p. 185
- Turkey Roll-Ups (contains a little mayo, can be substituted), p. 163

Appendix 2:
Recipes That are Useful for
Sneaking More Green Vegetables
Into Your Diet

One of the things that has had a noticeable impact on how I feel, athletically perform, etc. has been regularly adding green vegetables to my diet. I've found that about 3-4 cups of "leafy green" or "cruciferous" vegetables makes me feel awesome. By contrast, I've noticed that if I eat an otherwise healthy diet, but skimp on greens, it has a noticeable effect on my energy and performance.

I've noticed that fruit has a tendency to mediate this effect (which makes sense, because fruit is fairly nutrient-dense). When I'm regularly consuming a few cups of berries, I can get by on 1-2 cups of greens per day.

But getting lots of greens in my diet seems to be the surest route to cause my body to brim over with testosterone and dopamine, so I make green vegetable consumption a priority.

Unfortunately, greens kind of taste like crap. They (usually) aren't terrible. They're just bland. They're also easy to skip by accident, because they're typically a side dish. And personally, I'm not really a salad guy.

The consequence of all this is that I've made it a priority to track down tasty recipes that incidentally contain certain kinds of nutrient-dense veggies, like broccoli, spinach, cauliflower, Brussels sprouts, etc. This allows me to get my daily greens without the need to have a tedious side of steamed broccoli with every meal.

I've managed to find a number of recipes that fill this role for me, all of which I've included in the recipe section of this book:

- Bacon Broccoli Salad, p. 183
- Bacon Brussels Sprout Slaw, p. 99
- Green Smoothie Example, p. 141
- Green Protein Shake, p. 147
- Hamburger Salad (fairly small amounts of spinach per serving), p. 103
- Orange Chicken, p. 131
- Amazing Fake Mashed Potatoes, p. 113
- Sauteed Greens with Mustard Sauce (this is technically just green vegetables with sauce, but the sauce makes it taste pretty tasty as a side dish), p. 171
- Turkey Roll-Ups (due to the small amounts of watercress), p. 163

I typically eat 2-3 of these recipes per day, and rely on them as dietary staples. If you dislike salad as much as I do, I hope you find them useful as well.

Appendix 3:
Recipes for People
who Miss Grain

A lot of people, understandably, have trouble cutting out grain- and potato-based foods from their diets when they go paleo.

In the short term, this is often a low-level form of biochemical addiction that the body and brain have developed as a result of regular high doses of glucose. After an adaptation period, this tends to go away (assuming the person doesn't "cheat" too much, and keep the dependency alive).

Additionally, a lot of us have developed emotional and psychological preferences for these foods that have nothing to do with physiology. These attachments are reinforced by cultural norms, like the fact that most breakfast foods in the U.S. are centered around grain (cereal, toast, pancakes, waffles, oatmal, etc.)

Carb-cravings in general are fine, and fairly easy to deal with, since most of us can just add in some fruit, nuts, sweet potatoes, or other carbohydrate-based food and perfectly fine. Likewise, a sweet tooth can be easily solved with fruit, honey, and even dark chocolote.

However, these foods don't satisfy the psychological and cultural habits we've developed over time, which can be surprisingly strong. So it helps to have some healthy approximations of the comfort foods that we've gotten into the habit of eating

Which is the theme of this humble appendix.

There are only a few recipes in this book that fit the bill. Namely...

- No-Fake-Flour Paleo Pancakes, p. 127
- Paleo Cereal, p. 157
- Paleo Oatmeal, p. 159
- Amazing Fake Mashed Potatoes (for people who don't eat potatoes), p. 113

...which doesn't seem like a huge number of options at first, until you consider the fact that most people only eat 2-3 grain-based foods as part of their regular routine.

For example, back when I was a grain-eater, I ate bagels for breakfast, pasta for dinner, and the occasional hamburger bun or tortilla at a restaurant.

It turns out that most of us don't actually have much variety in our diets when we sit down and look at what we really eat on a daily basis. So four recipes should be enough to scratch your itch if you ever get cravings for grain.

Appendix 4:
A Few Simple Food Recommendations
That Don't Merit Recipes

The following foods are all ones that I eat on a regular basis, but due to their simplicity, putting them in the recipe section would a be a little silly. Because of their simplicity, they tend to be snacks, side dishes, etc, rather than full meals.

Many of these require zero preparation, which makes them great to whip up when you aren't willing or able to make normal food. Many of these foods are also great for travel or general on-the-go eating. For these reasons, and for just rounding out my diet in general, I find these foods very useful and enjoyable.

Almonds and Cheese - A mouthful of almonds and a bit of cheese is a tasty combo, and very portable. I like to take a small block of cheese and about half a cup of almonds with me when I go to a coffee shop to get some work done, and it makes a nice snack.

Apple Slices and Cheese – See above.

197

Deli Meat and Cheese – See above.

Green Apple with Almond Butter, or **Banana with Cashew Butter** – I've found that these particular fruit/nut butter combos have very complementary tastes. Just dip the fruit in the nut butter and enjoy. A little messy, but delicious.

A lot of people also like celery with nut butter. I'm not a fan of celery personally, but ants-on-a-log is an option

Grilled Asparagus – When grilled in a generous coating of butter, this is pretty palatable as far as green vegetables go, and very nutritious.

I typically eat this with chicken breasts or steak; I pan fry the meat first, then use the still-hot pan to cook the asparagus. Quicky, easy, and very healthy.

Steak - Obviously awesome. Making a basic steak is relatively straight-forward (steak + a little seasoning + frying pan). But if you want to get a little more elaborate, there are all kinds of cool marinades out there that work really well with steak, including some interesting ones based on things like citrus fruits or coffee.

The only downside is that steak can be pricey depending on what cuts you buy, and it's not suitable for batching. But if you can get around those obstacles, steak is very healthy, fairly easy to prepare, and (of course) delicious.

Sweet Potato Fries with Guacamole – Just use the guac the same way you would normally use ketchup (or whatever you normally dip fries in). Scrumptious. I use pre-made frozen sweet potato fries – the brand is Alexia, and they come in a bag in the freezer section of most grocery stores. If you have an aversion to pre-prepared foods, making your own sweet potato fries from scratch is relatively simple.

Turkey Slices and Mustard – I buy thin-sliced turkey at the Whole Foods deli. I've tried various types of mustard, and I'm partial to honey-mustard, but brown mustard and dijon mustard both work well.

Unflavored Greek Yogurt + Anything Flavorful – I've mentioned this elsewhere, but it's worth including here for the sake of completeness.

To flavor the Greek yogurt, I use either raw honey and almond butter, or a flavored whey protein powder (typically chocolate).

The honey-almond-butter option tastes better, and contains only whole food ingredients, while the whey option is helpful for getting extra protein in your diet, and can be made low-carb if you're so inclined.

There are tons of ingredients you can potentially mix in with the yogurt as flavoring, (fruit, cacao powder or dark chocolate squares, various spices, etc.) so use your imagination.

One-Ingredient Snacks and Back-Up Foods

- Various nuts (I'm partial to almonds and walnuts)
- Various seeds (sunflower seeds are a popular choice).
- Various types of deli meat (choose minimally processed meats like ham, turkey, and roast beef over processed meats like salami).
- Dried fruit (keep to a minimum)
- Jerky
- Hard-boiled eggs

A Brief Word
About the Author

"Sean Robertson" is the pen name of a lazy paleo enthusiast who prefers to remain anonymous on the internet. In real life, his interests include paleo food and writing about himself in the third person.

Okay seriously, this book has been a fun project, but I have no particular interest in creating a reputation for myself within the paleo community. I just want to offer some (hopefully) useful advice, sell a few books, and go about my life in the real world in relative peace.

If anyone wants to get in touch with me for some mutually-beneficial purpose (such as a blogger who would like me to write a guest article for their blog, a podcaster who would like to do an interview, etc.), I've set up an email address specifically for inquiries related to this book at LazyPaleo@Gmail.com.

Please note that as much as I like to try and help people, I don't have time to give personalized advice to anyone via email (nor do I consider myself particularly qualified to do so, since I don't know anything about you).

Likewise, if any readers of this book would like to argue with me about something I've written, tell me I'm a bad person, etc, I'd like to point out that I typically delete these types of emails after about five seconds. Which means that anyone attempting to bother me via email will have wasted much more of their own time than mine.

That being said, if you have anything nice to say, please feel free to drop me a line. I like nice people.

Most importantly of all – thank you very much for taking the time to read my partially-coherent thoughts on this topic. I sincerely hope you enjoyed the book, and that you'll continue to find it useful for years to come.

Sean Robertson

Made in the USA
Lexington, KY
14 March 2012